The Metabolic Museum

The Metabolic Museum

Clémentine Deliss

HATJE
CANTZ

Inside the museums, infinity goes up on trial.

Bob Dylan, “Visions of Johanna,” 1966

Table of Contents

Prologue

A few years back, some close friends encouraged me to apply for the directorship of an ethnographic museum in Germany. At first, I was cautious. I had been working independently as a curator and publisher for more than twenty years, traveling from city to city to set up new projects with artists, and I was keen to retain my autonomy. At the same time, I needed to settle down and transfer my experience onto an environment I could qualify with my own model. I was selected for the job and moved to Frankfurt, where I lived for five years. This is the narrative of my endeavor to transform the modus operandi of a contentious genre of European museum and develop a post-ethnographic institution.

Sometimes renamed museum of world cultures, the ethnographic museum is the most extreme rendition of a cultural institution that retains "colonial presence" even today.[1] While I focus on the crisis of this particular museum, I hope to address other types of venue that hold collections and recognize the necessity to rethink their constitution in the twenty-first century. If museums have to be pioneering and fight against routine, habit, and conservatism, what model of critical and reflexive methodology can be deployed on existing, forgotten, soiled, or non-restituted collections?

The subjective, dialogical activity undertaken in collaboration with artists, designers, writers, anthropologists, and lawyers at the Weltkulturen Museum between 2010 and 2015 consolidated the modus operandi of my earlier transdisciplinary curatorial practice. In Frankfurt, I sought to generate movement within the museum's institutional structure, affecting how we worked and where the priorities lay for a museum, both internally and toward the public. Located in three nineteenth-century villas, our *domestic research* centered on the tens of thousands of artifacts and the vast photographic archives housed within the museum.

This book was written in great part while I was a fellow of the Wissenschaftskolleg zu Berlin, the Institute of Advanced Study in Berlin. Practically airlifted out of Frankfurt, I was given a room of my own, safeguarded from inquisitive journalists, and encouraged to write up this experience as if it had been my own fieldwork in the museum. With the help of my notebooks, I was able to reconstruct the logic of each resolution that I took on a day-to-day basis until that day in April 2015 when the city of Frankfurt unfairly dismissed me.

I am grateful to the many friends, colleagues, and allies who supported me both during and after my time at the museum. In particular, I would like to thank Michael Oppitz most warmly for having faith in my approach and for accompanying me when my professional world fell apart; Paul Rabinow for his friendship since the mid-eighties when we were both in Paris, his guidance from afar, and his incisive and inspiring work around the concept of remediation. From the perspective of art practice, I thank all the artists and writers who trusted me as a curator, keen as I was to divert them from any banal orthodoxy of institutional practice by drawing them into unforeseeable situations and encouraging conceptual work with these sensitive and vital collections. In particular, I would like to highlight the stimulating and inspired collaborations that took place in the museum with Buki Akib, A Kind of Guise, Marie Angeletti, Farzanah Badsha, Benedikte Bjerre, Rut Blees Luxemburg, Peggy Buth, CassettePlaya, Marc Camille Chaimowicz, Sunah Choi, Hamish Clayton, Clegg & Guttmann, Minerva Cuevas, Mathis Esterhazy, Patricia Falguières, Heather Galbraith, Bryce Galloway, Gabriel Gbadamosi, Matthias Görlich, Werner Herzog, Pramod Kumar KG, David Lau, Armin Linke, Antje Majewski, Tom McCarthy, Tina Makereti, Markus Miessen, Shane Munro, Gabi Ngcobo, Otobong Nkanga, Peter Osborne, PAM (Perks and Mini), Francis Pesamino, Simon Popper, Ciraj Rassool, Olivier Richon, El Hadji Sy, Syafiatudina, Luke Willis Thompson, David Weber-Krebs, and the many art students of the Städelschule who exhibited in the Weltkulturen Labor's Green Room.

Lothar Baumgarten, James Clifford, Hans-Jürgen Heinrichs, Peter Pakesch, Dan Peterman, Issa Samb, Teimaz Shahverdi, Sebastian Schellhaas, and Richard Sennett were trusted interlocutors who accompanied me while I tried to fine-tune new relations between museum collections and contemporary meanings. Finally, I would like to show my respect to the many friends in Frankfurt who helped me through various phases of this journey, in particular Ann Anders, Rüdiger Carl, Konstanze Crüwell, Jutta Ebeling, Uwe Fischer, Susanne Gaensheimer, Bärbel Grässlin, Tamara Grčić, Raphael Gross, Wolfgang Günzel, Nikolaus Hirsch, Phyllis Kiehl, David Hofferbert, Michael Hofferbert, Stefan Mumme, Yvette Mutumba, Alexandra Papadopoulou and very Frankfurt, Philippe Pirotte, Tobias Rehberger, and Bernd Vossmerbäumer.

Manifesto for the Post-Ethnographic Museum
Frankfurt/New York, October 2013

Anomalous and anachronistic:
It's about working with a collection
that belongs to another time
that belongs to other people
that is deeply connected to the histories
of European colonialism and trade
that is contested and will continue to be contested
whose potential for referentiality is far from expended
whose restitution is undeniable.

Domestic research:
It's about working with existing architecture not against it
moving between apartments, studios, archives, and labs
finding structural solutions for the installation of artifacts
repositioning collections both conceptually and physically.
It's about rethinking possibilities
of research inside a museum
through self-critical and recursive inquiry
slow, prone to change, not always visible
reintroducing a laboratory into the practice of a museum
developing new assemblages based on historical collections
building a workshop for the production of prototypes
constructing an exhibition out of this continuing procedure.

Remediation over time:
It's about daring to change
the anthropological classification of the collection
suspending the *logos* of *ethnos*
and earlier organizing principles:
region, religion, ethnic group, culture, society, and function
developing alternative metaphors through dialogical research
healing a deficient situation
shifting medium, enabling interpretation.

Curating neighborhoods:
It's about inviting artists, designers,
lawyers, writers, historians,
and anthropologists in residence
those who connect to the original source of the collection
those who come from elsewhere
rubbing shoulders through their engagement with the collection.
It's about making rooms available to visitors
encouraging the public to usurp the museum
to shelter in it, study, and meet
taking in exhibits through the corner of one's eye
fully deploying the educational brief of the museum
checking the open access digital studio.

The Museum-University:
It's unequivocally collection-centered
working outward from actual exhibits
deconstructing earlier archives
and histories of ethnographic museums
introducing external impulses,
an epistemological generalism
a democratic intellect
a non-standardized education
as independent as possible
providing a new platform for professional development
connecting the next generation of global cultural protagonists
from curatorial studies, cultural studies, postcolonial studies,
contemporary art, design, performance, art history, anthropology,
creative writing, law, ecology, mathematics, and more,
breaking open the disciplines of the past and their collections.

Walking Through

In the period leading to my move to Frankfurt, I walked through as many ethnographic museums in Europe as I could. I wanted to witness their status in contemporary civil society, understand the contradictions evoked by their outdated modes of display, and learn more about the power structures behind the inordinate mass of artifacts held under lock and key. I began by focusing on the immediate constituents of the museum experience. I sought to match the body of the visitor with the corpus of the collection and the broader metabolism of the museum. I wondered in what manner members of the public move through an exhibition. How long do they engage with the displayed artifacts? What is the relationship between seeing, feeling, and thinking? Are they provided with a chair purposefully placed in front of a vitrine for lengthier contemplation? Or do they stand upright as if facing a screen, ready to swipe on, and rarely moving closer or bending down to peer at the underside of an exhibit? At the British Museum, a guard told me of the fainting fits and panic attacks he witnessed, regularly forcing him to give up his chair. This was the public's biggest complaint: that only one small bench was available to sit on in a room with an expansive exhibition.

The museum as a spatial configuration of inhabited meanings adapts only very gradually to change. Timing is a curatorial unit, place is clearly demarcated, artworks are hung according to norms, lighting and air humidity are coordinated with conservation requirements. Visitors readily accept this monitoring environment, which anchors and regulates their perception. If a video is projected, there may be the opportunity to lie on a carpeted floor, slump on a mattress, or find a stool to sit on. Hours can be spent in this way because new media are recognized as requiring a longer period of intake than a painting, photograph, sculpture, or set of artifacts. Robert Harbison noted in 1977, at a time when video works began entering the museum, that the "immersion in the object that stops time is achieved by treating it as an existence to be lived in rather than something to be stopped in front of or looked at, and one can almost tell from people's movements whether they have entered a painting or are only staring at it."[2]

The bias against the body of the spectator dates back to the European Renaissance, when architects and designers saw the gallery as a "fixed theater of spectatorship" intended "to regulate strictly the viewer's range of motion and object of focus."[3] As museum spaces gradually evolved over the course of the eighteenth century from private house museums into public institutions, those "unruly social bodies" who once engaged in "flirting, playing, eating, drinking, talking, laughing, and napping" on ottomans, benches, or at tables, were gradually evicted.[4] By the early twentieth century, the curatorial trope became one of "disembodied opticality," whereby seating no longer featured beyond a short stop-off point along the scenographic route through the museum. Indeed, with the advent of the white cube environment, the fear of a "reembodiment of the spectator" works to rid rooms entirely of any means of repose or study, leaving only banal exit signs to indicate the "intrusive" presence of human biology.[5] As Diana Fuss and Joel Sanders explain, "art's visual consumption owes much to the flow-management philosophy of department stores, which rarely provides seating in the main shopping areas. A seated patron, after all, is not likely to be a consuming patron; consumer culture requires bodies on the move, not bodies in repose. Simply put, the bench is anathema to the capitalist space of the modern museum."[6]

Today, the museum—now hygienist—is obsessed with its own dirty data, cleansing and disinfecting its contaminated past, particularly the bloody residue attached to the traumatic memories of slavery, colonialism, and the Holocaust embodied in its collections with their absent proof of legitimate provenance. Collections have become the toxic witnesses to genocidal practices.[7]

Forms of human engineering in museums accelerate and support the necropolitical constitution evoked by Paul B. Preciado when he speaks of the museum becoming "a semiotic-social corporation where immaterial goods are produced and commercialized."[8] "What bodies can the museum institution legitimate?" he asks. Whatever they are—national histories or artworks—they become pawns or foot soldiers in the battle for sovereignty. The museum, writes Preciado, "is a factory of representation" that supports the "social prostheses of the royal body on which its sovereignty is built and negotiated."[9] Identifying Preciado's "somatopolitical" dimensions of the museum leads back to the corpus of the museum and its sequestered collections. Here organs generate meanings under excessive structures of containment, built from that which Ann L. Stoler so succinctly defines as "imperial duress" that is, the effects of "pressure exerted, a troubled condition borne in the body, a force exercised on muscles and mind."[10] For Felwine Sarr and Bénédicte Savoy, ethnographic objects are the "bearers of a reserve of the imagination as well as the material manifestation of forms of knowledge (*savoirs*). Fishing nets that encode algorithms from fractals to anthropomorphic statues in passing by amulet-filled vests: the work of decoding the various forms of knowledge they conceal as well as the comprehension of the epistemes that have produced them still remains largely a work to be done.... It is indeed a question of re-activating a concealed memory...."[11]

Yet is this dialogue possible when the magnitude of artifacts, including their referentiality to colonial collecting practices, is quite literally impounded underground? Held in inaccessible storage units, belongings acquired, looted, or wrenched away in the name of science, trade, or diplomatic exchange are sedated and safeguarded through their juridical, carceral inscription within the annals of an other's institution. In the never-ending ethnographic present, anthropologists, both then and now, continue to reflect the image of the slave onto their interlocutors from other cultures, erasing the individual identities and intellectual property rights of the artists, designers, and engineers whose works they acquired or looted.

Today we are faced with the "incalculability" of the act of restitution.[12] As a result, the public exhibition with its tightly coordinated displays actually works to tame the tension inherent in these sealed-off storage spaces, as if the custodians were dealing with a feral, uncontrollable energy yet to be exploited. How else can one explain the elaborate retention strategies that work to prevent access to the contents of these depots? Such vast inaccessible holdings of ethnographica can be read as multiplex organizations of material ingenuity waiting to be re-encoded within today's contexts, needs, and realities. The constellation of artifacts in a collection, each with its inevitably creolized imprimatur, rejoins the condition of today's visitor who searches among numerous iterations of difference for that singular sensation of conceptual intimacy. As such, the public needs to experience exhibitions as multiperspectival reflections on the museum itself, its disputed collection, and its position within European history. On June 2, 2010, I wrote, "How can we know the intentionality behind an object without named and documented authorship? Can we empower the new observer to create an additional and nonexclusive interpretation? We don't want a cathedral. We aren't representing foreign policy. We can dare to articulate the possibility for confusion."

At the interview for the job, I laid down my concept. It was still in development, but the key issues were clear to me. The new model for the museum would be the house itself, a renewal of a domestic environment of repose and reflection, of living, dialoguing, researching, and production in contrast to a corporate site of consumerist culture. I would introduce a laboratory into the museum, and initiate new inquiry along with international artists, writers, photographers, filmmakers, and lawyers, who would live and work quite literally in the museum. The door would be open to anthropologists, too, but the invitation was directed mainly toward outside disciplines and practices. Every selected object would generate printed matter referencing both historical records and new interpretations. By then I knew that I wanted students to work in the museum, we would set up an evening school, and there would be fellows with long-term affiliations.

Over the course of the interview, I was asked a rota of questions. Could I develop a concept for a new building and permanent display; what did I think of the current exhibition on the Sepik; how could I manage crises among personnel; and what would I do to make the museum more attractive? That day, I visited the museum in preparation for the interview and jotted the following notes:

> Too much information on the walls and all in German; clutter hidden behind cardboard structures that act as decoration; blue linoleum laid onto the original wooden parquet flooring; no authentic photographs, only reproductions; stuffed animals presented alongside ethnographic artifacts; simulated installations that pretend to represent anthropologists at work; rubber plants dotted in different parts of the exhibition presumably to evoke a tropical atmosphere. The museum has gone to seed.

I began to recognize the museum as a complex body with a severely ailing metabolism, afflicted organs, and blocked channels of circulation. To transform this condition would require careful nurturing, but also radical operations. It was Issa Samb, the late Senegalese philosopher and founding member of the Laboratoire Agit-Art who provided me with essential guidelines for the task:

> To work in the ethnographic museum, you have to begin with an inversion. You need to exhume the objects and place them at the forefront again. This will constitute the first level of analysis, the first reading. Then walk through the interior of the museum. Don't start to classify anything yet. Just walk, look, and name the directors who preceded you and recognise their bias. By criticising their bias, you will begin your work. Today, every person who directs an ethnographic museum will need to proceed in this manner in order to help ethnography advance quietly towards its status as a science. In the world today, meanings for such sciences need to be redrawn, or it will always be the same. So, leave traces, mark your presence. It's only in this way that all these objects will supersede their aesthetic status and finally retrieve their human dimension. You will be able to socialize each object that you find and, in doing so, you'll restore life to them. No object in a museum is a useless

object. Each one can elucidate proto-history and sociology. In reading them, one acquires a facility to understand the present. If you come across a prototype, isolate it straight away and give it a new number below the initial one. Prototypes change. Ethnographic museums confused culture with civilisation, human beings with their objects. Every person has a culture. Civilisation is a fabrication. You will need to make corrections here, corrections to notions of modernity and classification. We need a critique of classification because classification contains the germ of racism.[13]

Artists and Anthropologists

I had visited the ethnographic museum in Frankfurt ten years earlier in the autumn of 1999 as the newly appointed guest professor at the Städelschule in Frankfurt. On one occasion, the dean of the art school, Kasper König, took me to meet the director of Frankfurt's department of culture. They both knew of my background in cultural anthropology and wanted me to take on the vacant directorship of the ethnographic museum. At this first meeting, I declined. It felt anathema to the excitement of teaching art students. A couple of months later, the director invited me back to his office. Again, I refused. The main reason for not accepting the offer was informed by my studies of anthropology in the mid-eighties. At that time, the subject of analysis was not the foreign culture and its artifacts so much as the figure of the ethnographer. Anthropology, the "maculate,"[14] soiled science, could be deconstructed by decoding the tropes employed to "write culture."[15] Neighboring literary criticism, post-structuralism, and psychoanalysis, this radical strain of semantic anthropology was barely engaged in defusing the charged condition of its founding institution, the colonial museum and with it, the hundreds of thousands of confiscated artifacts. Studying anthropology and art practice in Vienna in the early eighties, I read everything I could that was brought out by German publishers such as Syndikat, Suhrkamp, or the Qumran Verlag. I discovered texts by ethno-psychoanalysts Paul Parin, Fritz Morgenthaler, and Mario Erdheim, essays by transgressive thinkers like Hubert Fichte, the work of Michael Oppitz and Fritz Kramer, alongside the more mystically oriented research of Hans Peter Duerr. This theoretical material played a role in the German-speaking art world of the time. As art students we read anthropology because there was little else. There were no formalized courses in curatorial studies and no transcultural academies; nothing but a relatively conservative art history, which bore little relation to the heteroclite practices of Actionism, Concept Art, and performance.

Key to this interdisciplinary crossover was a text written in the seventies by American artist Joseph Kosuth titled "The Artist as Anthropologist."[16] In a sequence of numbered paragraphs, Kosuth cites economist Michael Polanyi, philosopher Martin Jay, sociologist Max Weber, and anthropologists Stanley Diamond, Bob Scholte, and Edward Sapir, and draws a map of contextual adjacency with which he aims to destabilize the narratives of Western modernism and scientism as the defining references in contemporary art. He argues for an "anthropologized art," "an art manifested in praxis," an "engaged" activity founded on "cultural fluency" whose criticality succeeds because it "depicts while it alters society."[17] Kosuth's article—with its typically male figureheads—was more than merely a reading list for emerging artists. His intellectual stance corresponded with the aftermath of the first Independence period in sixties Africa, emancipatory movements in the US, the global student demonstrations of 1968, and the fallout of the Vietnam War. The relationship between contemporary art and cultural anthropology was built upon the articulation of linguistic and contextual propositions that might activate a recursive adjustment to ways of understanding and representing art itself.[18]

As a doctoral student in anthropology I was required to do fieldwork, so in 1986 I moved to Paris to investigate the storage rooms, archives, and ephemera of the Musée de l'Homme. I wanted to establish a link between those concentrates of Concept Art and Actionism that I had witnessed in Vienna as a young art student and the edginess and subversion that I detected within certain strains of twentieth-century anthropology. I named this connection *eroticism*, less with reference to gender studies or sexuality, but as a philosophical drive that motored both the ideational extremes of artistic research and various experiments in ethnographic inquiry. One afternoon at the Musée de l'Homme,

I came across the incomplete collection of the dissident Surrealist periodical *Documents* (1929–31) edited by Georges Bataille and Carl Einstein. Here I recognized the *prelusive* moment, the uncertain and unresolved phase in creative practice, and its ability to activate entry points beyond explanatory or contextual forms of information. I decided to juxtapose the written and visual assemblages in *Documents* with the collecting activities of the team of French anthropologists who crossed Africa between 1931 and 1933 on the notorious Mission Dakar–Djibouti, amassing more than 3,500 objects for the Musée d'Ethnographie du Trocadéro in Paris.

The thesis was a handmade affair produced on discs the size of a bathroom tile and interspersed with black-and-white photocopies of archival material. I asked an artist friend to take photographs of me while I worked in the museum's library, standing on steps to reach books, or holding a Dogon mask on my face against the backdrop of metal filing cabinets.[19] Alongside these self-portraits, we took photographs of Michel Leiris in his office or in conversation at the museum's Le Totem bar. All this led to a doctorate that stuck out from the purely text-based, literary dissertations of the time. By then I had realized that academic anthropology was not my future. It was the summer of 1988, and I was keen to return to art and become a curator. The new discipline of cultural studies was flourishing in Birmingham under the leadership of Stuart Hall, and the Black Arts movement was active in London. Rasheed Araeen was preparing the seminal exhibition *The Other Story* and Black Audio Film Collective and Sankofa were producing films on the Black experience in Britain. In contrast, the Museum of Mankind in London's Burlington Gardens felt both disconnected from movements in contemporary art or cultural studies, and out of sync with curatorial practice.

The artists who made an impact on me as a student often worked in relation to a form of meta-ethnology. I focused on Lothar Baumgarten and his friend the anthropologist Michael Oppitz, who in turn was close to Marcel Broodthaers, Benjamin Buchloh, and Candida Höfer. Baumgarten and Oppitz created a shared wilderness out of their early expeditions to the Pitt Rivers Museum in Oxford. In 1976, Oppitz headed to Nepal to begin his long-term visual and textual recordings of Magar shamanism.

Two years later, his friend abandoned the relative security of the Rhineland art scene for the Orinoco in Venezuela, armored with "a machete, a towel and a change of clothing, two Leica cameras, some film stock, a tape recorder, batteries, watercolor paints, pens, and paper."[20] Both messed with the sanctity of documentary material in different ways, testing out the poetics of chance encounters and alternative representations in language and visual media. Whereas Baumgarten's adventures held fort within the discourse of art, Oppitz strode a high-wire suspended between the authority of academic publishing—that "paper persona" he always refused to become—and the experiments he performed in visual anthropology. His commitment to fieldwork was not one of rugged individualism in search of personal enlightenment, but a desire for human exchange.[21] He questioned what it meant to be part of a context, be it in time or space—in Kathmandu, Cologne, or Kassel—in contemporary art or in anthropology. Is it one's physical location, one's political stance, or one's interlocutors and the conversations they engender, he asked? Or might it be the desire to identify an emancipatory nerve, an organic alliance to those whose positions lie outside of the institution, thereby keeping the unforeseeable nature of the human condition, and the archival drive that defines it, both alive and contradictory? Oppitz recalls the period:

> When you look at historical situations now and what was going on in Düsseldorf and Cologne between 1968 and 1975, there was something of a movement which we participants were not aware of at the time. All of us who were part of it thought, Jesus, we live in the wrong time. If only we had lived at the time of *Minotaure*! If only if we had lived during the Mission Dakar-Djibouti, we would be happy! There would be a bigger self. Now if we look back at this situation—and I talk to younger people about this—they say, damn it, why didn't we live in 1968–1975 in Cologne and Düsseldorf! There were a number of people who you could see forming a group, although they weren't. They didn't understand themselves as such. The Surrealists did see themselves as a group for a short time, and they had a leader who kept them together, and there were people who created

> the ideology of the group. In Cologne and Düsseldorf, we did not have lead figure. There was maybe this or that artist who was a little more attractive than another one, and of course there were people whom we would not consider at the time, like Otto Piene or artists we found totally uninteresting. As time goes by, distances become larger and then it looks even more as if it was a group of self-made alliances.[22]

With its philosophical heritage, Frankfurt was a prominent player in the conversation between art and anthropology. Central to this junction of minds was the publishing company Qumran Verlag (1980–85), conceived and directed by writer and anthropologist Hans-Jürgen Heinrichs. With his connections to Parisian publishers and Swiss intellectuals, Heinrichs was the first to offer translations into German of French ethno-poets Victor Segalen and Michel Leiris, and to dissolve the barriers between genres by bringing out new texts by writer and traveler Hubert Fichte. Eroticism, possession, mythologies, the oneiric and the irrational all merged with an alternative history of ideas that found an avid readership among anthropologists and young artists alike. Limited edition box sets with photographs of ephemeral artworks drawn in the sand by Joseph Beuys in Kenya, or depicting murals by Papisto Boy, a graffiti artist from Senegal, were sold at leading art bookshops and information galleries. Like its contemporaries, the Merve Verlag in Leipzig, Jean-Michel Place in Paris, or Semiotext(e) in New York, Frankfurt's Qumran Verlag reflected a collective interest in transgressing linguistic, aesthetic, and political borders by highlighting the subjective sensibilities of transdisciplinary knowledge production. Although Qumran lasted a mere five years, as an organ for writers and artists it laid the foundation for a far-reaching debate between advanced anthropology, literature, psychoanalysis, and contemporary art.

A year before Qumran folded, Josef Franz Thiel, the director of Frankfurt's Museum für Völkerkunde, commissioned the thirty-one-year-old Senegalese artist and activist El Hadji Sy to curate a new collection of Senegalese paintings and works on paper for the museum. I had visited this German ethnographic museum in 1992 when I was preparing the exhibition *Seven Stories about Modern Art in Africa* for the Whitechapel Gallery in London.[23] At the time, it was the only institution in Europe that held a considerable number of drawings and paintings by named twentieth-century artists from East, West, and Southern Africa. Sy's work was seminal in Dakar. He was a founding member of numerous artists' collectives including the Laboratoire Agit-Art and had pioneered a notorious studio complex in the center of Dakar that was violently disbanded by the Senegalese military in 1983. Sy was renowned for having dedicated ten years of his life to painting with the soles of his feet in reaction to the Senghorian paradigm of visual art and state representation.[24] Nineteen eighty-four was not only the year when Sy was commissioned to assemble a collection of contemporary Senegalese painting for the museum, but also the opening of the much-disputed exhibition *Primitivism in 20th Century Art*, curated by Kirk Varnedoe for The Museum of Modern Art in New York.[25]

At the time, this synchronous double take on art and ethnography located both in New York and Frankfurt would have been barely perceived. Whereas the MoMA show pretty much dug its own grave by epitomizing a myopic relationship between African and Western art, the Weltkulturen Museum gave free rein to a Senegalese artist, effectively the first curator from Africa to have worked with a European museum. Aware of the need for serious art-critical reporting on contemporary art practice in Africa, El Hadji Sy also coedited a trilingual anthology on art production in Senegal with a foreword written by Léopold Sédar Senghor, former Senegalese poet-president and close friend of Pablo Picasso and Pierre Soulages. The book also included a text on art criticism in Senegal by Issa Samb, aka Joe Ouakam.[26] With Sy's anthology in hand, I was able to locate him in Dakar and subsequently invite him to become one of the five African cocurators of *Seven Stories about Modern Art in Africa*, which opened in 1995. Described by Nigerian novelist and dramaturg Wole Soyinka as "unique in a number of ways," and the "harvest of a creative journey that began on the African continent," the exhibition was a complex conflation of modernist painting and post-independence movements, supported by a team approach to curatorial work.[27] It was the precursor of subsequent exhibitions and acted as a launch pad for some of its cocurators.[28] Today, Sy's contribution to the history of Senegalese painting and the development of independent artists' movements in Dakar warrants greater attention, both in terms of academic analysis and regarding his considerable work as a painter. Wilful omission is a procedure no one likes to talk about. It can take on different scales, morphing according to whether it is generated by a politician, an historian, a scientist, a lawyer, a curator, or a journalist. All too often, ethnology and art history work through the medium of omission, provoking consensus through the presupposition of a common reasoning that either extracts something or withholds key dimensions from a narrative.

In 2010, I invited Sy back to Frankfurt to reflect on the collection that he had curated in the eighties, and provide additional and complimentary information to the inventory cards. Because several artists of his generation had died in the interim, this return was fraught with emotional memories. At the time, the person responsible for the museum's African collections did not adequately record or take notes on Sy's oral history. This experience would prove an alarming precursor to the widespread resistance to recognize alternative and legitimate meanings generated by artists in relation to a museum's collection. Several decades following Sy's pioneering work for the Frankfurt museum, I was able to engage the Afro-German art historian Yvette Mutumba to become the new curator of the museum's African collection. Her detailed knowledge of contemporary art from Africa and its diaspora outweighed the standard expertise of most ethnographers or area studies specialists. By 2014, Mutumba had identified more than 1,400 works in the museum's collection, significantly helping to restore the value of individual authorship to a collection that, in its generic taxonomy, had been founded on the disenfranchising discourse of ethnicity. Once more, we invited Sy back to the museum, and with the legacy of Fritz Axt's art collection that he had inherited and generously lent to the museum, Mutumba and I were able to mount a retrospective of his practice as painter, performance artist, and activist.[29] For five years, the Weltkulturen Museum in Frankfurt would become an experiment in venue construction, intended to articulate not only the dissident approach of these earlier countercultural artists and anthropologists, but to consider how new relationships between collections and methods of inquiry might be nurtured by artists within this post-ethnographic institution.

During the first month, I organized a series of internal roundtables with the curators of the regional collections. I was curious to understand their involvement with the university. Were they invited to teach seminars or lecture? Did they have students, or give classes on museum ethnology? I discovered that in Frankfurt the rift between anthropologists at the university and those who worked at the museum was historically and emotionally charged.

From 1925 until the late sixties, every director of this city's ethnographic museum was automatically the head of the well-endowed Frobenius Institute, which sat within the campus of the prestigious Goethe University in Frankfurt. However, something had gone afoul between the two institutions and, after much acrimony, they were divided. The museum was sidelined to the municipality, like a public knowledge bank and object crypt, whereas the university institute could afford to do pure research, garnering academic accolades and funding with a minimum of teaching or public mediation. Both venues held collections, which had been severed during the divorce. Photographs taken during fieldwork expeditions to Africa, for example, were kept at the university, while the items they related to were stored in the museum's depot. This separation was unwieldy and only served to stymie any new research into the archives of both institutions.

For *Object Atlas. Fieldwork in the Museum*, the first exhibition I curated, artist Thomas Bayrle succeeded in extricating works on paper by his father, Alf Bayrle, painted during a collecting expedition to Ethiopia in the nineteen-thirties led by Leo Frobenius and held in his homonymic institute. We exhibited the elder Bayrle's gouaches and drawings with the original stone steles that had been in the possession of the museum for nearly a century. To move and install these megaliths in the museum gallery involved renting a crane. One can only try to imagine the outlandish schlep incurred to bring these carved effigies to Germany from Ethiopia. These stones, weighing hundreds of kilos each and incised with the traits of different phallic heads, had been uprooted from their respective sites in former Abyssinia and brought to Frankfurt, an extreme act of dislocation comparable to mass identity theft committed by a German provincial city. The memorial presence of ancestors for an entire community had been obliterated and their gravestones uplifted, regardless of what the reverse act might have implied within a European context.

From what I could make out, the division between museum and university centered around two main issues. Firstly, the decolonial developments of numerous countries in the early sixties that brought with them a necessary critical shift in social anthropology from its earlier twentieth-century focus on ethnographic artifacts to more immaterial subject matters. Research collections, once avidly gathered to elucidate non-European cultures, became less central as heuristic tools of scientific speculation. Anthropologist Paul Rabinow describes the situation in the nineteen-twenties as follows: "the museum's scientific role consisted of promoting technical and sociological studies of objects and peoples cast broadly within a Maussian *fait total* (total fact) perspective in which each object was illuminated by—and metonymic of—a whole society."[30] For Marcel Griaule, the leader of the French Mission Dakar–Djibouti (1931–33), to understand the background to the 3,500 material artifacts forcefully removed from the African continent was to come one step closer to mapping the indigenous mind.[31]

It was not until the advent of Structuralism that Claude Lévi-Strauss could shift the debate onto immaterial fields of knowledge. As he stated in a lecture presented to UNESCO in 1954, it was now more relevant and far easier to study the languages, belief systems, attitudes, and personalities of other cultures than to acquire their bows and arrows, drums, necklaces, or figurines. A second reason for the division between the museum and the university was more mundane—the occupational status of anthropologists in ethnographic museums in Germany was traditionally that of a functionary or civil servant and not a university professor. Even if the museum staff harbored ambitions in the arts and humanities, this situated condition of employment promoted an uncomfortable hierarchical and disciplinary division that I wished to address. Like a muscle that had lost its traction, I hoped to revitalize the research arm of the museum, adding value to the museum's output beyond the required quota of public footfall.

To an outside observer, the Weltkulturen Museum was dormant. Most citizens had visited it only once, as children. This stagnant condition was not a special case, but the reflection of a systemic institutional and political condition that I found in equal measure in the twenty or more *Völkerkunde* (ethnological) museums in Germany's provincial cities. Their respective holdings referenced families of artifacts sourced in inordinate quantity on expeditions and then swapped between museums to fill any gaps in their encyclopedic collections. Together with the restorers and conservators, the custodians demonstrated an affective connection to artifacts that lay within their area of cultivation. They had favorite objects, beloved villages or regions, and preferred certain cultures and practices to others. They chose to speak on behalf of these, using a language derived from their studies at one of the many institutes of ethnology in Marburg, Mainz, Göttingen, Cologne, Frankfurt, or elsewhere in Germany. Evidenced by a feeble level of postcolonial reflexivity or readiness to engage in transdisciplinary inquiry, the monoculture of ethnological museums began to resemble intellectual plantations.

Coming from the outside as I did, these schools of museum ethnology constituted a tight network of colleagues and peer groups that was remarkably resistant to external communities of researchers, and particularly to artists. As the first weeks passed, I began to sense the complexity of my position within the museum. If I felt legitimate as the elected director, I could tell that my intellectual and academic identity was foreign matter. Within a short space of time, the partition of competence became clear. I pointed out that I would not compete with the curators' regional and contextual knowledge of the objects in the museum's stores, but like all previous directors, I staked a claim to another know-how, in this case curatorial practice and contemporary art. Every time I took an artist through the depots, I could be sure that they would identify something unresolved. Out of the corner of their eye they would spy an object lying on the top of a shelf, locked away and ignored. The presupposition of exoticism was actually alive in the stores of the ethnographic museum. You only needed someone from the outside to activate a search. Later, when we undertook fieldwork in the museum with guest artists and writers, artifacts that had been neglected by custodians for years were seen, touched, and gradually inserted into a critical and experimental process of remediation.

At times, I thought about the death of the ethnographer, as if the departure of this expert on other cultures might constitute the breakdown of this institution. If one museum ethnographer passed on, then so too would their simulacra of voices, ventriloquating on behalf of others. I wondered whether it was just I, as a professional, who was so resistant to the authoritarian discourse of the ethnological museum? What emotions did lay visitors encounter when they entered a museum of *mankind*? How did they come to terms with the affects generated by this artificial procedure of squeezing every dimension of another life into units and comparatives? Displays were intended to make the public feel transported to an originatory space and time, and the visitors' book was full of comments along the lines of "Where are the Red Indians?" or "My daughter misses the exhibit on the Pygmies." Grotesque as these inscriptions appear today, such preconceptions are harbored by the genre of the ethnographic museum, whose role has been to enlighten, enchant, and mystify at the same time.

In 1992, while he was president of the International Council of Museums, the former president of Mali, Alpha Oumar Konaré, valiantly suggested that all museums in Africa be "killed" in order for a new approach to culture and heritage to flourish.[32] Can one ever succeed in revalidating an institution that has colluded with the violence of colonialism? Might this be achieved by reevaluating research collections, and insisting on their access and visibility? To this purpose, I changed the designation of the museum's staff from that of curator to *research curator* in the hope of motivating a new era of conceptual inquiry and collection-centric prototyping. I would apply the concept of remediation, developed by Paul Rabinow, in a humble, reflexive attempt to heal the injuries and occlusions of the past.[33] This methodology, recognized within advanced anthropological circles, would require the introduction of alternative media and modes of representation in order to activate a process of regeneration and redesign. "The core idea," writes Rabinow, "is that concepts arose from and were designed to address specific problems in distinctive historical, cultural, and political settings. When the settings change, and as the problems differ, one cannot take these things up once again or simply reuse them without changing their meaning and efficacy." This procedure, which necessitates teamwork, is a dialogic and recursive condition through which certain practices are "reconfigured, modified, rectified, and adjusted." However, such remediation is necessarily hostile to the "nostalgia (or worse) of an unconditional allegiance to tradition." It focuses instead on the reformulation of the contemporary, "an orientation that seeks out and takes up practices, terms, concepts, forms and the like from traditional sources but seeks to do different things with them from the things they were forged to do originally or how they have been understood more recently."[34]

By gathering artifacts into new assemblages, one would activate taxonomic transgressions, clashing entrenched identifications and highlighting the underlying structures of power generated by listings, narratives, visualizations, and omissions, dating from different periods and authors. Earlier monographs drafted by anthropologists and experts from area studies would still be central to contextualization. Testimonials from the original producers and users of these artifacts so rarely recorded or documented, would remain paramount. However, all these interpretations would need to be expanded with contemporary readings that crossed disciplines and instituted a new constellatory mapping, or object atlas. Extending Aby Warburg's system of the *Mnemosyne Atlas* onto three-dimensional phenomena was a way to disconnect existing denominational and classificatory systems, or at least to place them into jeopardy. To articulate the complexity of the museum through its collections would necessitate a curatorial methodology that explored different propositions, be they aesthetic, art critical, cultural, historical, scientific or personalized. One approach to this decolonial dialogue would be through experimental exercises between artworks with recognized makers and artifacts with undocumented authors, both being subject to discursive procedures of allocation, evaluation, and marketability.

In 1990, I had curated an exhibition for the Steirischer Herbst in Graz, which included selected works by neoconceptual artists alongside various items purchased in markets in West Africa.[35] *Lotte or the transformation of the object* was a response to the formalist anachronism of the New York Museum of Modern Art's 1984 exhibition *Primitivism in 20th Century Art*, and a critique of the naïveté of *Magiciens de la Terre* held in Paris at the Centre Pompidou and at La Villette in 1989 and which opened the floodgates of the Eurocentric art world to the numerous axes of global art production. At the time, I was interested in the crisis affecting ethnographic museums in Europe. In parallel was another debate: the suppression of art-critical interpretations that engineered a discursive closure around the reception of contemporary art from the African continent. Catalogues produced in the nineties more often omitted the art criticism written by Africa-based intellectuals and writers.[36]

To articulate this lacunae through an exhibition, I drew in different commodities made from mass-manufactured objects, which I garnered from markets in Kumasi, Freetown, Abidjan, and Ouagadougou, but equally from other commercial spaces such as galleries including Jay Gorney Modern Art in New York, and Max Hetzler and Gisela Capitain in Germany. This juxtaposition was a ruse based on formalist friction aimed at drawing attention to the failure of Western museums and curators in the late eighties to recognize and respect art-critical and academic positions from the African continent. I sought to align the undocumented ethnographic artifact with the Readymade, and recast this modernist tension in the context of early Institutional Critique. The exhibition indirectly referenced the nonexistence of the named artist in European ethnographic collections. As a result, all the exhibits in the *Lotte* exhibition, including works by Haim Steinbach, Jeff Koons, Mike Kelley, Rosemarie Trockel, and Lubaina Himid were presented in the exhibition without wall labels. Today, it would be practically impossible to omit references including not only the name of the artist, but also that of the gallery (or galleries), agents, and coproducers. In the early nineties, this experiment in visual thinking deployed artworks and artifacts on equal level in order to throw light onto the narrow referentiality of an art world suddenly confronted with alternative modernisms and a new geo-aesthetic cartography.

By the turn of the millennium, curating had developed into a booming academic discipline that extended earlier museum studies once taught in provincial universities to include master's courses on exhibition histories and a burgeoning multilayered critique of ethnocentricity. But this new complexity to exhibition making had not evolved at the same pace within European ethnographic museology. Britain and France quickly airbrushed over the predicament, cutting down on custodians and research facilities by centralizing their respective collections. In London, the Museum of Mankind celebrated its upgrade to the grandeur of the British Museum and in Paris, Jacques Chirac created his own "secret garden," a monument and memorial to the cultures of the world designed by architect Jean Nouvel. Germany lagged behind but banked on its construction of the Humboldt Forum in Berlin to enter the club of state-funded, universalizing museums. By 2010, the typically DIY style of ethnographic exhibitions had been superseded by an entire industry of interior architects and exhibition designers, who also played their hand in the mises-en-scène of department stores. The Cologne ethnographic museum, Rautenstrauch Joest, reopened following an extensive refit by a leading German firm costing several million euros that came replete with interactive tables designed in pseudo-Rococo style, silky white fringed curtains to veil ritual objects from too much inspection, and elaborate wall texts, all there to perversely compensate for the absence of contemporaneity and legitimacy surrounding this ethno-colonial institution. The gamble was that these costly makeovers would provide a smooth transition into the twenty-first century and help to address new audiences. We were back at the capitalist aesthetics of the emporium.

For the first six months, my work consisted of preparing a spatial concept for the museum's new extension. A small park area situated behind the three historical villas had been designated as the site for an annex that was to measure between 5,000 and 6,000 square meters. The decision to build on that specific spot had been taken by the city magistrates long before I arrived. Remarkably, this set of interconnected back gardens with their unruly bushes and tall trees became the focus of an emotive citizens' movement, which succeeded in halting the museum's plans and the city's ambitions. The direct neighbors mobilized the residents of the Sachsenhausen district and beyond, managing to rustle up several thousand signatures in opposition to any construction in the gardens. It was claimed that the designated architects would cut down more than forty trees, and that the city would lose a vital urban park, substituting it with a museum that no one really wanted. The media enjoyed the controversy, stoking it further so that when Frankfurt's department of urban planning let slip that the new building, notwithstanding the impending arboricide, was to cost more than eighty million euros, the city's magistrates quickly voted against it and the project was shelved. This had been the third failure in the museum's recent history. In the eighties, two attempts, including one by architect Richard Meier, to create an adequate exhibition space for the city's beloved ethnographic collections (that no one had really seen) also fell through.

I sensed a dead duck from the start of my term, but I somehow believed in the relevance of this museum. Indeed, how could a city like Frankfurt, whose unique selling proposition was its internationalism, lose out on a museum with a collection spanning the world? What could such a museum signify in the third millennium? Moreover, what type of critical operation might succeed in bridging the racialist ethnology of Germany's past and today's transversal conversations? How could one activate the collection within an intersectional debate, when the environment of the museum itself was housed in architecture corresponding to the colonial period? The museum was literally as old as the villas, which were constructed between 1890 and 1904. This parallel accentuated the urgent need for redefinition; for finding the appropriate discursive closure to this compromised institution. In 1939, when the Allies bombed the original site of the museum at the Palais Thurn und Taxis, destroying two thirds of its collection, the remainder was transported by car to over a dozen private homes and castles in Germany. The interim director moved the museum's administration to her home in Frankfurt's bourgeois Westend district. Karin Hahn-Hissink worked there for thirty years doing mainly administrative jobs, such as revising the inventory cards and stamping them with *Kriegsverlust*, or war loss.

In the early sixties, a team of museum anthropologists scoured the Sepik river in Papua New Guinea in a bout of salvage anthropology returning with 4,000 artifacts, but no museum building to exhibit them in. In 1969, Hilmar Hoffmann, Frankfurt's director of culture, allocated the first of three historical villas on Schaumainkai to the homeless yet expanding ethnographic collection as part of his master plan to create a "Museum Shoreline." However, the collection remained dispersed until the mid-eighties, when it was finally transported to its current location: a six-floor concrete bunker connected to an electricity transponder for public transport systems. Inside, an industrial lift took you literally around the world, moving slowly up and down each continent like a huge, steel Faraday cage the size of a small room. Each floor represented another region. Seventy thousand unauthored artifacts from the past were held in this concrete container, invisible to the outside and barely decipherable from within.

The building saga continued, and months were spent refining briefs and conceptualizing the rooms of a new museum that would—if I were not vigilant—become normative and stagnant before it had been constructed. Looking through my notes of the time, I realize how many people I was able to mobilize to help me steer the course for what I named a *post-ethnographic* museum.[37] The city's director of culture would warn me repeatedly that the building was not "mine," could not be designed for "my" direction, but had to surpass any individual concept and take on a neutral position, effectively becoming a museum like many others, only better. These are the words that I spoke on December 16, 2010, to the international jury that chose the winning entry for the new Weltkulturen Museum's building:

> Writing as early as 1915, Carl Einstein, the German theoretician of African art contemporaneous with Walter Benjamin and Aby Warburg, claimed that museums were the foundation for living schools. For Einstein, collections reflected the extremes of intellectual exploration and if kept mobile through juxtaposition and contrast, could provide museums with essential energy. If not, he warned, they would become mere "preserve jars," and "anesthetize and rigidify into a myth of guaranteed continuity, into the drunken slumber of the mechanical." Einstein's position is analogous to the notion of the "democratic intellect" proposed by Scottish philosopher George Elder Davie (1961), who believed in the potential for every citizen to develop a generalist understanding of the world by combining visual culture with the natural sciences, and Northern with Southern philosophies.
>
> Nearly one hundred years later, the challenge of the Weltkulturen Museum in Frankfurt is to remain sensitive to past histories while inventing practices and assemblages for future generations. Today, fieldwork no longer takes place on journeys to distant lands, but within the museum itself. And it is in this sense that the design of our museum has to reflect the kinds of expeditions we can undertake today, and the stories we hope to tell in the future.
>
> With the new building, we are faced with the challenge of remediating the museum's outstanding collections and presenting the wealth of ingenuity that resides in these objects that have been collected from all over the world over the last one hundred years.

But what do I mean by remediate? First, to remedy something: for example, the ambivalent resonance of the colonial past. Here we need to develop something like a post-ethnographic museum, for we are no longer depicting *ethnos*, the tribe or grand anthropological themes through examples of material culture but taking these extraordinary objects as stimulus for future innovation and therefore the starting point for new knowledge production. To remediate also means to bring about a change of medium, to experiment with other ways of describing, interpreting and displaying the objects in the collection. Here we recognize the value of introducing the Weltkulturen Labor into the museum, both as a physical location for inquiry and as a virtual extension of communication.

The laboratory is about testing out new concepts and methods. Guest artists, curators, and scholars are invited to live and work in the museum. During their residency they select objects and images from the museum's collections and produce new ideas, texts, or artworks from this experience. They also conduct seminars with students and give public lectures. Our first guests are Antje Majewski (February 2011), Thomas Bayrle (March 2011), and writer and anthropologist Hans-Jürgen Heinrichs. And we are currently in discussion with DJ Spooky, Otobong Nkanga, John Akomfrah, Pablo León de la Barra, Dan Peterman, Martin Kimani, Dieter Roelstraete, and Werner Herzog. The laboratory also houses our new program for young museologists who come from Peru, Mexico, West, South, East Africa, New Zealand, etc.; in other words, those locations that connect to our collections.

The Weltkulturen Labor, which is a central concept of the Museum, fuels a domestic cycle of living, studying, working, and mediating. An outside-inside-inside-outside process that feeds new ideas gleaned through the collection into every event, exhibition, and publication.

I believe that our new building should be a macro version of this domestic cycle, expanded to accommodate a large audience who can make use of the museum to meet, talk, look, think, become inspired, study, sit down, return, spend time, and regenerate both their lives and the museum itself.

The Weltkulturen Museum is about people, objects, and their trajectories. For objects, too, are migrants, and embody partial or incomplete knowledge. The design for the new building should reflect the inherent tensions of our societies, recognizing that the museum offers less a static endpoint than a dynamic moment of connection in an ever-fluctuating assemblage of identifications between people and things. Frankfurt as an international trade route becomes the central axis of a contemporary form of cultural and civic circulation.

The museum sits in a landscape: botanically and physically it is situated in our park. But it also relates directly to questions surrounding the international culture of museum architecture today. This museum is no exception. And yet, we do not need to follow the trend and replicate another mega-museum building or iconic monument that insists on consumption and waters down open-ended forms of inquiry and experimentation. Such a construction sits uncomfortably in these times of recession and ecological awareness.

Perhaps what we should look for instead is a series of pavilions, stations, or satellites, which connect together to produce a circuit that promotes flow. Visitors may find different functions within these satellites with their contrasting atmospheres: in one they can look at an exhibition, in another they can read and study for several hours at a time, in a further location their children take part in an educational program, and in another, they meet to debate.

It is a museum campus, with the dynamics of social, aesthetic, and political discourse located within a metaphorical courtyard, as can be found in West African villages.

So we leave behind the museum as emporium, that nineteenth- century ritual precinct modeled on large-scale Victorian department stores. Dioramas with mannequins and the old tension between being either an art exhibit or an ethnographic mode of presentation are not part of this museum. The department store museography with its

> creeping class differentiation that we find in so many world culture museums is not appropriate for our aims.
>
> Instead we want to demystify these objects, dissolve their aura of anachronism, and with the help of guest artists and scholars begin to identify new prototypes within the collection. Moving through the main exhibition space in the new building with its adjacent reading room is the Reservoir, with its extensive public study collection and conjoined auditorium with another temporary exhibition space. Here, we can provide a setting for these ingenious objects which makes them accessible to future generations, who see them as capital, as generative of future designs and who are ready to recognize the correspondence between how they were once used and how they can be made to work today. Innovation energizes the museum's exhibitions such that visitors immediately identify *Weltkulturen* with twenty-first century ideas and questions.
>
> To conclude: I hope that our analysis of these architectural designs will culminate in a courageous selection, one that moves away from constructing yet another big corporate museum, a club sandwich of a building that sits heavy and stretches deep underground, and instead towards a lighter, archipelago model of interconnected islands in the park, characterized by an inherent sense of mobility that favors the visitors' potential to project their lives, their histories, and their aspirations into this new museum, the embodiment of a migratory architecture of human experience.

At the final stage of the competition, which following European rules was based on the anonymous participation of nearly fifty architectural offices, it became clear that one design would win. The plans for an underground museum topped with a glass cuboid entrance appeared to resolve the problem of interference within the grounds of the urban park. Given the proximity to the Main river, the water level could pose a threat, but this aspect was played down. Instead, the politicians saw a new world cultures museum that would be inoffensive to the point of disappearing. I cannot say that it was my favorite plan, but it was made clear that

I had no choice. From the same evening that the jury's decision was made public, the citizen's movement began its aggressive campaign. A few days later, I wrote an email to James Clifford, who was a member of the selection committee: "The press conference went really well. But since then, the citizens' initiative has gone berserk in the press and claimed that all forty trees in the park will have to be felled. Some scientist has been doing Google Earth mappings and come up with loopy theories about the winning entry."

The process of developing a new museum space was challenging, but I never felt dependent on its resolution. Instead the three villas—however incongruous to museum activities—actually embodied the architectural elements that would transport my concept of *domestic research.* Built at the turn of the nineteenth century, all three villas had been homes to banking families. In the early nineteen-forties, the larger villa, which we used for exhibitions, was transformed into an orphanage and later into a school for young women preparing to enter "domestic professions." The museum's administration and curatorial staff worked in the adjacent house, which was styled in a Gothic genre with pointed turrets. The third villa, built in a Classicist style, had been used by the local police department. People still spoke of it as *die Polizeivilla* (police villa), which may have accounted for the ugly frosted windows and neglect of its original features. All three villas had a multitude of kitchenettes, which were used for staff recreation. Over the years, the original bedrooms, drawing and dining rooms had been recast to misshapenly serve various museological functions. In one of the cellars was storage space for more than 13,000 historical artifacts from Africa. Inaccessible to the public, this basement was a warren of small locked rooms filled with wooden school cabinets containing piles of folded textiles and stacks of small objects including pipes, jugs, mugs, figurines, baskets, and textiles all made from organic materials. The place smelled of a mixture of cowhide, fermented milk, and citric moth repellent. One large surface was littered with miscellaneous artifacts that could not be classified other than as "unidentified." They lay there waiting to be provided with an inventory card and allocated a drawer or cupboard to sit in. In five years, I cannot confirm having seen any alteration to the constellation of items on this table.

The exhibition space was in dire condition. Nearly all the windows had been sealed off with plasterboard. Fake walls foreshortened the original layout's curves, and spotlights from the eighties hung from tracks nailed to the ceiling. The former director had gone so far as to puncture the original wooden wainscoting that ran along the oak staircase leading up to the belétage and insert pointless small halogen lights. Streaky blue linoleum covered the parquet floors, apparently meant to simulate the trajectory of the Sepik river in Papua New Guinea, and the museum's retail outlet resembled a charity shop with a jumble of world crafts and discount publications. Next door, in the museum's public library, encyclopedias of tropical birds, redundant foreign language dictionaries, and outdated tomes of "Who's Who?" filled the open stacks alongside obscure ethnographic journals. With surreal opening hours starting at 7 a.m. on certain weekdays, this polymathic archive with more than 50,000 publications and periodicals from around the world was a ghostly reminder of twentieth-century bourgeois drawing rooms with their class and gendered erudition. It represented an anachronistic shrine to the selective interests of German schools of ethnology.

I was concerned with rendering the dysfunctional library active again, updating the periodicals and breaking the self-imposed seal to the outside world. The designer, Uwe Fischer, helped me to remodel the shelving into a new configuration more conducive to browsing and reading. With hired assistance, the librarians gradually transferred the volumes of encyclopedias to the basement and filled the empty shelves with *General Anthropology*, a heteroclite category that gives this discipline its truly Bataillesque character. Publications with no apparent connection to one another were placed side by side: a treatise on Bantu languages written in English in the mid-twentieth century rubbed shoulders with an analysis of scarification and a more recent publication on postcolonialism and sport. The library's system of classification was neither arbitrary nor was it personalized and idiosyncratic. Here like elsewhere, it followed the rules dictated by German library norms. It was impossible to ascertain the logic behind the resulting constellations of themes and languages or neighborhoods between authors with the result that the rubric of general anthropology became about as unidentifiable as the groupings of anonymous artifacts in the museum's collection.

I decided to redirect the remit of the library away from themes inherited from nineteenth-century anthropology toward contemporary aesthetic practices, cultural studies, and literature. This did not exclude more traditional monographs on specific societies or art styles, but it sought instead to provide a broader discursive range in line with exhibition developments and the individual research interests of the guest artists and scientists. I cleared out subscriptions to obtuse journals, ordered *Third Text*, and purchased the archive of the seminal Qumran Verlag. Qumran's publications numbered more than one hundred and included collaborations with Francis Bacon, Michel Leiris, Max Raphael, and many others. It was not only an example of ingenious late twentieth-century interdisciplinary publishing, but it helped to legitimize my continuity of the museum's original focus on the symbiosis of art and anthropology. If it had not been for the intransigence of the librarian's profession, we might have created new visual reading routes between the racks of world literature. Other dimensions to the museum necessitated endless bureaucratic correspondence and meetings with city officials. I was informed that Frankfurt was a notorious hub of classified information and that as a municipal institution, the museum was on a par with the city's prison. The department of culture participated in this paranoia, with the result that the museum staff could only access the Internet from their offices.

While these time-consuming administrative moves were being deployed, I began relocating the image archive from the first floor of the laboratory villa to the basement. Josef Franz Thiel, a former director of the museum and missionary by profession, had established the archive in 1987, recognizing the potential of photography for ethnographic analyses. But by 2010, the image archive, like the museum library, was being used primarily by staff for personal research, to illustrate talks, or find material for an exhibition they were working on. Located across several rooms, the image archive contained more than 100,000 photographs and 500 recordings. Metal cupboards lined the walls of the villa, distributing the weight so as not to crash through the floorboards. Large tables were covered with scatterings of slides, bits of paper, and trays of miscellaneous documents. Two men labored under broad daylight, meticulously digitizing photographs at extremely low resolution. One of them would hold a thirty-five-millimeter color slide up to the window and attempt to decipher its contents. Another trailed disenchanted through an unclassified stream of archival data. Incongruous photocopies of guinea pigs and birds were pinned to the walls and piles of unfinished projects filled the shelves.

I persuaded the city to let me take on a young graduate anthropologist who was keen on getting involved in the museum. Deftly, she extracted as much knowledge as possible from the archivist and accordingly classified and packed the thousands of slides, glass plates, negatives, and prints, transporting them from the villa's first floor into the basement. There she sorted them into different areas and set up a special room dedicated to the museum's large archive of missionary photography. Her perseverance helped to make the laboratory into an active multimedia resource. Artists and writers-in-residence could move freely between the top floors where they slept and worked, down to the laboratory and image archive. Everything was in-house, accessible day or night, which significantly facilitated the development of ideas and interdisciplinary production in the museum.

Unexpectedly, fifty percent of the image archive consisted of studio photographs of artifacts in the collection taken between 1960 and 2009. These objects were rarely shot in situ. Instead collecting expeditions focused on rapid mass acquisition in the knowledge that visual reproductions and textual narratives would be produced once back at base in Europe. To have halted on a collecting expedition could have led to complications. For example, the seller might become curious about the buyer's intentions and their interest in a particular artifact. In-depth inquiry would take too long and run the danger of raising the price or potentially persuading the seller not to relinquish this object of desire. Moreover, if an overly thorough documentation were produced on site, then what would be left for the museum ethnographer to do back at the museum? Their professional raison d'être was not only to exhibit the booty in Germany, but to couch it in their own expert words, evaluating it according to museological norms.

Gradually, the ethnographic collection with its exoticist heterogeneity transformed into the opposite: a pedestrian series of household articles with the defining characteristic that they had not been made in Europe. Other more ritual artifacts, now relocated in Germany, also lost their original mana. To counterbalance the devaluation generated by the voyage from the tropics, a particular genre of studio photography became common currency, not only in ethnographic museums but also in auction catalogues and publications of so-called tribal art. Artifacts were choreographed within an atmosphere of engineered darkness enhanced by spotlights and evocative gritty colors, boosting what was now missing from the object, and thereby producing its necessary commodification. The orphaned artifact was made to look precious, patinated, unique, and priceless.

I knew immediately that I could not work with the dominant visual discourse of museum anthropology. How could I interest anyone in a critical reappraisal of these collections, if I resorted to the same primitivist clichés? As an antidote, I engaged Wolfgang Günzel and Barbara Rademacher, Frankfurt's leading exhibition and art photographers, to portray every aspect of the museum's activities as well as re-shoot those artifacts that had been singled out by guest artists. This allowed me to chronicle the studio set-ups of visiting researchers, document their assemblages of artifacts in the laboratory, as well as record all the public events that took place in the museum, including lectures, evening classes, and exhibitions. Rather than focus on the masterpieces in the collection, for which scores of photographs existed already, we photographed only those items selected by the external artists and researchers, always shooting them from a similar angle with neutral lighting against a sterile white background and void of additional atmospheric ingredients. This presentation, which inevitably evoked another visual discourse, that of contemporary art and its white-cube aesthetic, nonetheless endowed the laboratory's activities with a clarity of intention, which contrasted with earlier processes of visual obfuscation largely intended to conceal the ethnographic institution's compromised history and authority.

One afternoon, the image archivist, who was going through quantities of unclassified transparencies, came across a cardboard box. It had been kept well hidden under a desk in one of the stores. The first set of images we found was of an embryo, conceivably dead when photographed. We searched further and uncovered more complex material, in particular hundreds of full-body shots of men, all naked and taken from the side, the back, and the front. The founding director of the museum had been a doctor, stationed on a Sumatran tobacco plantation in the eighteen-nineties in the service of the German colonial authorities. His posting involved treating unskilled migrant workers who suffered from all sorts of skin diseases and illnesses due to the effects of noxious pesticides. As a scientist and physician of his era, Bernhard Hagen was interested in racial typologies. His job in the colonies provided him with an unanticipated comparative paradise. He set up a makeshift studio on the plantation and began assiduously photographing all the migrant workers who came from countries as far apart as Afghanistan, Sudan, China, India, and Malaysia. In addition to these worrying full-body shots, annotated with the person's ethnic origin but not their name, we came across approximately fifty black-and-white prints of close-ups of male sexual organs, taken in the same location. Later we uncovered missionary archives with photographs of female genitalia shot in Africa in the late fifties. One of the custodians mentioned the "loneliness of being a missionary" but I chose to let that comment pass. We had indeed revealed the archival underbelly of the museum.

In the past, the museum had accommodated these collections by deferring their necessary critical and reflexive analysis—basically occluding any knowledge of such archives. In order to problematize this photographic material, I ran three seminars in the Weltkulturen Labor. We needed to talk about how to handle and exhibit these controversial and disturbing images. With artists Clegg & Guttmann, Armin Linke, Otobong Nkanga, Antje Majewski, and Luke Willis Thompson and guest anthropologists in particular Michael Oppitz and Markus Schindlbeck, we discussed the objectification of people in the racially deterministic photography of German ethnology. In parallel, we questioned the anthropomorphic and affect-driven photographic renderings of artifacts collected by ethnographic museums. Otobong Nkanga reacted forcefully against the use of imagery in ethnological analyses, stating that, "the fragmentation of the human body in photography was a scientific tool to get closer to the object and to probe. It's about penetrating a space that should not be penetrated," she added. "We feel the violence of the camera, which becomes like a prodding stick."[38]

German ethnographic photography played a significant role in the debasement of personhood, and this forensic model applied to the physiognomy of artifacts as much as it did to humans. Artifacts became humans, and humans were reduced to objects. Nkanga visited the museum several times to do further research, photographing Central and West African currency, weaponry, and jewelry as she held it against her body:

> I come from a background in performance, and with these photographs I consider the relation between the body and

> the objects. I'm not interested in revealing the face of the person holding the artifact, because here the focus is on the connection between the object, its size, and the human body. By removing the white gloves and showing skin, the viewer can relate to where the object might have come from and to the idea of a black population. I want to think about who I am making these photos for. To remediate is to give information back to the younger generation. Photography helps me find a way to talk about this heritage without having to adopt a pedestal or a stage.[39]

This unexpected result of fieldwork in the museum became the foundation for the exhibition *Foreign Exchange (or the stories you wouldn't tell a stranger)*.[40] Frankfurt had been at the center of international trade for over nine hundred years. Fairs, which functioned as a junction for the traffic in foreign goods featured ahead of the banks and as early as the eleventh century. In the sixteenth century, Germany set up trading posts or "colonies" in Ghana, Venezuela, and the Amazon region. Trade colonies and protectorates grew in scale at the end of the nineteenth century with the official entry of the German Reich into European imperialism. Mercantile incentives intersected with scholarly research such that the museological assemblage of ethnographic objects could be seen as a side product of commercial interests. Speaking in 1904, Bernhard Hagen, the first director of the museum, emphasized the relationship between trade and knowledge. He wrote: "Our German Fatherland has evolved from a major power into a world power, and German trade and commerce now has large, indeed massive interests in all five continents. What did China, let alone Japan mean to a German merchant only 50 years ago? Today, every large manufacturer or merchant must bear these empires in mind, not to mention the Australian and African markets ... A slight upset in a remote corner of East of Asia may trigger the most severe stock market crisis here. Now this is a gap not yet filled by the geography of trade. This is where the new science of ethnography comes into play."[41]

If one assumes that underpinning all collections are the traces of former trade routes, and if one takes the metaphor of tracking and mapping one step further, then it is curious to consider how historical collections may come to represent either a continuing flow or an impasse. For how should one treat those areas within colonial or imperial collections that are not updated? Are these perversely the artifacts whose public exchange value, visibility, and presence-engendering capacities are being repressed? An example of such a collection is found in the armories of eighteenth and nineteenth-century universal or encyclopedic museums. How can one update this assemblage of weapons to include the kind of warfare technology (including food security measures) that we hear about through the media, that is purchased through middlemen (both public and private), and that constitutes a commercial enterprise, which is neither discussed nor exhibited for the cultural edification of the wider public? Similarly, collections that reflect highly nationalist identifications such as those found in folklore have become redundant as reflectors of urban-rural identities in today's worlds. The trade routes and civic identifications that underpinned their reasoning have shifted. Today, the mediating role of the museum operates within a different dynamic.

Let's assume that a person who moves from one part of the world to another brings with them a set of objects in their suitcase. The transition to a new environment alters and shifts the architectonic frame within which these things once found their place. Their owner has to renegotiate the presence of these goods within a new social experience and spatial practice. This is an activity of adaptation and adjustment, which helps to resignify meanings and affect between people, objects and places.

An ethnographic museum introduces a further dimension of agency in this relationship, one that is incorporated in the person of the anthropologist or collector. Between the movement from there to here, from say the Amazon to the city of Frankfurt, ownership has altered from one of reasonably straightforward personal possession (as above) to one of ambivalent custodianship. The object is no longer housed in the home, on the market stall, or placed on the ritual altar relative to its faith of origin, nor is it transported in a suitcase as a personal souvenir. Instead, it passes through a process of reconstruction that involves internment, administration, assessment, and conservation. The ethnographer as collector is now in the middleman position and turns out to be the person who generates legitimacy and history around an object or, chooses not to, denying presence or seeking to enhance this potential. In short, there are institutions, which act as trading posts and there are the middlemen or brokers, who negotiate exchanges of knowledge between groups and individuals. The rules of the game may vary and the scale will reflect different economic, cultural, and political incentives relative to state, municipal, or private ownership or custodianship. Visibility is not always guaranteed—the broker may be illegal, or the institution may wish to obfuscate its engagement with regard to this transaction.

If we take on the possibility that individuals and groups from dense, working-class neighborhoods can wish to make presence in the cultural centers of the city, then the position of the middleman raises interesting questions. For there is no sole legitimate trader of perceptions. There is the itinerant hawker whose method may be chaotic, informal, part of a nonaccountable administrative activity and most probably linked to a complex set of aesthetic practices more or less under the radar. The broker may also be rethought within cultural centers as an artist, an architect, a designer, a visitor, but also as a building: a museum with a collection, a house that can engender intermediation. As Philippe Descola wrote in 2004, when describing the Musée du quai Branly, *Le musée un grand trafiquant d'agences*: the museum is a huge trading post of agencies. I would argue that trade and trafficking turns the museum into a temporary home, a sheltered space, a *maison de passe*, even an half-way house with all the shades of activity one might associate with this nomenclature, locations which can be usurped by visitors and citizens without entry or exit examinations.

The first artist to walk through the stores with me was filmmaker Werner Herzog. I hoped he might curate an exhibition, maybe even the first. The museum collection covered all the regions where Herzog had directed films, from Ghana to Brazil, Venezuela to Alaska. Within six hours of writing to him, he replied, offering to visit the museum in early May 2010, on his way back to Los Angeles:

> Dear Clémentine Deliss, your proposal sounds interesting to me indeed. It is a strange coincidence that I have been planning—since quite some time—to create a series of films on dying languages and the last speakers of these languages around the world. This is a cultural imperative in my opinion. It is true that almost all Völkerkunde Museums are gathering dust, and no one knows what to do with them. To re-conceptualize them is long overdue. Your idea to check out the Magazin is something I have contemplated myself, as there are surprises quite possible, but I think it should not be pre-arranged in conjunction with places I have filmed in. If there is someone who knows the contents of the Magazin well, I would like to encourage this person to just dig into things wherever there is a sense of wonder. I have filmed a first round in the Ardèche region already, and I have to return there on Wednesday. Best, Werner Herzog.

A few days later I wrote:

> I shall collect you from the airport and we shall go straight to the main storage space. I reckon we shall stay there for an hour maximum, until around 7pm. The museum custodians are preparing a small selection of objects for you to look at that they feel signify a sense of 'wonder.' (The theme you suggested has sparked off interesting debates within the museum and we are holding a roundtable next week to discuss it ahead of your arrival). I think this should give you a first impression of what may be possible. Then we will visit the museum's villas on Schaumainkai. We shall be renovating the exhibition villa beginning in October 2010. This will involve getting rid of unnecessary false walls and restoring the original features. But you shall still have a chance to see how much potential this small, charming villa has. Right next to the museum is a discreet Austrian restaurant. If you are not too tired, perhaps we could have something to eat? The Frankfurter Hof where you are staying is a walk across the bridge over the Main, five minutes maximum.

His reply arrived within a few hours:

> After finishing the cave shoot, I decided spontaneously not to fly back to the USA, and return a week later for Warsaw, Berlin, and Frankfurt. Right now, I am in Styria, and for e-mail coverage I have to drive up a mountain. Your plans for Frankfurt sound quite reasonable, and I am looking forward to the museum with great curiosity.

The custodians were professional and friendly as Herzog walked around the storerooms. He enjoyed glimpsing objects between the rolling storage cabinets and coughed loudly when the moth repellent became too intense. He got into handling the throwing weapons with no qualms or gloves, and none of the custodians stopped him from doing so. He told me several times that he never went to museums, and that he had not made an exhibition before. He knew nothing of the shows that I told him about, such as Massimiliano Gioni's 2008 *After Nature* at the New Museum, or the 2006 exhibition with his work at Blum & Poe in New York, and was surprised that these shows related to his film production had taken place without his knowledge. After his visit, I wrote the following notes in my diary:

> May 11, 2010. I have just taken Werner Herzog back to the hotel. He stands in the lift with its golden walls, a small cube, jewel-like, and he thanks me, pressing the button to ascend. We have just spent six hours together exploring a sense of "wonder," to find out whether the museum has objects in its collections that can provide truths beyond human ingenuity, phenomena that speak from algae to rocks through an intelligence that transcends the limits of what we know and are able to recognize. He was shown artefacts from the regions of the Amazon, Peru, Bolivia, and Alaska, from the Sepik, Papua New Guinea, Micronesia, Australia, and from the Congo, Cameroon, Zimbabwe, and Nigeria. By the time we reached the Africa collection housed in the cellars of one of the villas, he was tired. But there was a strange leather belt, something inexplicably woven, "folded algebraically," he said, which caught his attention. Later in the restaurant, he told me that I would be surprised by the things he would suggest. He liked the Sepik orator sculptures, the ones that look like stools but are not. Instead the narrator leans against their carved body and in so doing evokes the ancestors, the previous orators and their words. He asked me about my background and latched onto my work on the Mission Dakar-Djibouti. As we had dinner, he stared at me whilst I spoke (I caught his gaze) and told me I should work on my diary, and that it didn't matter what others had written in the 1930s or later. I asked him whether he would consider writing a scenario for an exhibition. He said, no. Emphatically. These things had to be kept quite separate, he reiterated. He could not imagine working with these objects as if he were filming a storyline. A film had to have narrative, but these objects could not be pushed into a storyline, he repeated. It was as if their past was too complex. Suddenly the museum artefacts that we had seen that afternoon felt so stubborn to me, like they were digging in

their heels, resisting transformation, refusing to move. It was strange to sense the orators' stools as if they were able to manifest resistance. Later on, we talked about intense situations on trips to Africa, his incarceration in Central African Republic when he was filming the documentary on Bokassa. And we spoke about cinéma vérité and *Les Maîtres Fous* by Jean Rouch, but it did not lead to where I had hoped. I mentioned Djibril Diop Mambéty, but he did not respond.

Dan Peterman was the second artist to visit the museum and stimulate the conceptual reworkings of the collection. Peterman had set up the Experimental Station in 2002, a multifunctional collective on the South Side of Chicago. The Station held regular debates on police misconduct and community politics, housed a number of self-sustaining businesses including a bike workshop, a farmers' market, and a printshop, and ran the appropriately named Invisible Institute for journalism. I had been to the place a couple of times before and hoped Peterman would visit us in Frankfurt. One day in July 2010, Dan and I began searching through the Africa stores. He wanted to look at weapons. I had been told that nearly a quarter of the museum's collection was made up of the paraphernalia of warfare. There were hardly any guns, but there was a large quantity of knives, daggers, clubs, bows, and arrows, and armory. As we left Africa and headed for Oceania and South East Asia, Dan turned to me and said, "You know, today conflict doesn't happen with weapons as we know them. It's shifted to food security." Immediately, our search took on another direction and we began investigating the multitude of fish traps and hunting contraptions from the Pacific Region, South America, Alaska, and Southeast Asia. With Peterman's optic we tunneled below the ethnographic classifications and their presuppositions on weaponry, relocating our investigation to the field of fisheries and agriculture, and unearthing a quantity of ingenious designs. Here too, we encountered the absence of documentation of the named engineers or designers of these traps. One could read the multiple layers of innovation in each of these contraptions, extending from their woven geometric structures to the calculation of their entry and exit holes and floating quality once placed onto water. These exercises of fieldwork in the museum had drawn items from the collection into a contemporary dialogue. Werner Herzog and Dan Peterman recognized the transformational capacity of the museum's collection if located in the present.

More recently in Chicago, artist Theaster Gates, who learned much from Peterman, has produced his version of the house-museum based on a regeneration of abandoned buildings, which he takes as the first stratification of the archive. Gates initiated his particular form of urban archaeology with Dorchester House in 2009, which he carefully restored and redrafted as a "home for discarded collections."[42] Since then, he has acquired further real estate and set up the Rebuild Foundation, the Archive House, the Listening House, the Black Cinema House and the Stony Island Arts Bank, funded in part through the sale of marble bonds inscribed with "In art we trust."[43] Gates's approach to realty in Chicago's South Side complexifies the gentrification incentives of the majority of initiatives in contemporary art that range from biennials to new museum buildings. He "alter-locates"[44] histories that have been frozen or forgotten, ranging from the rebuild of a Huguenot house in Kassel (for Documenta 12), to the presentation of ceramic works by a former slave whose anonymity acts as a synecdoche for the exclusion of Black authorship by colonial powers. Along with his ongoing engagement at the University of Chicago, he develops more freestyle structures in the same neighborhood based on discarded real estate and obsolete collections which he transforms into an educational index for the twenty-first century. For Gates, artists have the capacity to "invent the platform." [45]

Jyotindra Jain, who initiated the National Crafts Museum in New Delhi in 1956, and which—remarkably—housed onsite studio spaces, once described certain museums in India as having been "pre-colonial." For Jain, this was a chronological term, implying that such venues were Maharaja museums, founded prior to British colonialism. They may have been "colonially informed," but their authority as institutions was not legitimized by the British administration.[46] Jain made a plea for the contemporary adaptation of the anthropological museum in the Indian context. "In India," he stated, "not collecting contemporary ethnographic material is to deny the present."[47] What might a contemporary ethnographic collection for a European museum look like, I wondered? Would it be the entire contents of a department store full of the world's functional items and luxury goods with their mixed cultural heritage, skewed authenticity, and multiple producers? Or had acquisition shifted from the earlier speculative and occult interests of anthropologists to the rising market in global contemporary art? If collecting for ethnographic museums in Europe had come to a standstill, which institutions were able to place a purchase on life's unknowns? In the past, these museums not only collected the everyday; they actively sought out representations of the unchartered, unexplicable, even the uncanny. The unforeseeable was part of their fascination with the Other, a bug-chasing desire to put one's status quo at risk. In the late nineteen-twenties, Michel Leiris declared that he would rather be possessed than talk about the possessed, and so he left Paris, rejecting the conventions and correctives of everyday life, and embarked on a collection expedition that would provide him with a transducer into the unknown. For Leiris, the world became an unpredictable, somatic conversation, both internalized and shared through collective experience.

I had begun to redefine the rooms of the three villas, redistributing activities that had lost their dynamic, prioritizing the domestic and the backstage as much as the public areas, and renovating the apartments. I imagined the museum as if it were a body, a metabolism built on the cohabitation and interchange between different organs with symbiotic functions. Renaming the museum "Weltkulturen" enabled the use of this umbrella noun to signify forms of interdependence ranging from lab work to exhibition making, running a researcher's club for teenagers, curating the Green Room for experimental exhibitions together with students from the Städelschule, and developing the digital Open Lab with a media agency in Frankfurt. The laboratory villa was the intellectual and aesthetic heartbeat of the museum, designed to restore an ergonomic rhythm to the critical apprehension of the institution and the artifacts in its possession. A circular arterial route provided each guest with an autonomous rota of day and night activities located between lab, studio, and apartment. The guest had no invigilator watching over them, or curator standing by to monitor their time in the laboratory. This process was new and there were ongoing discussions with the regional curators, varying in intensity according to a wide range of preferences and personalities.

The museum had never hosted so many heterogeneous yet qualified researchers before, and this required a readiness for dialogue between inside and outside expertise. The healing procedure affected not only the remediation of contested collections but every dimension of the institution itself. The *post-ethnographic* laboratory, which opened at the Weltkulturen Museum in February 2011, represented a differentiated, transdisciplinary space of inquiry. Post-ethnographic indicated that it recognized its historical underpinnings in ethnology but sought to transform this discipline by introducing a panoply of alternative forms of know-how, including art, that would help to critically draw out the ramifications of this colonial discourse. The laboratory venue was neither the depot, with its cold, uninviting atmosphere and rigid regional classification of artifacts, segregated and secured in locked storage units; nor was it the exhibition environment with its public entrance, watchful museum guards, and conventional opening hours. If the depot was about specialist closure and the exhibition about mass accessibility, this laboratory needed to offer an alternative spatial and conceptual configuration. I might have simply called it a workshop.

When I was a small child in the sixties, my parents, who had moved to London, ran two shops called *DELISS*, one for making clothes and the other for making shoes. They had taken out a lease on two neighboring town houses in Beauchamp Place, a Georgian street in Knightsbridge, close to the department store Harrods. The house at No. 40 Beauchamp Place spanned several stories. The ground and basement floors were designated as shop areas open to customers. The first floor was set up for designing and pattern cutting; the top floor for sewing and finishing. You could buy garments off the peg or order your clothes based directly on my mother's seasonal collections. The shoe shop was similar: six craftspeople from Cyprus and Jamaica produced made-to-measure shoes by hand, but also boots, bags, belts, and other accessories. There was a small stockroom, piled high with a myriad of colored leathers, suede, and reptile skins, which had a distinctly archival quality to it. My father trailed the leather wholesalers in Bermondsey for unusual handpainted or patent leathers. Apart from the shop floor with its eccentric window display, clothing racks, mirrors, changing rooms, and comfortable seating, everything else was about private innovation and production. My mother would work in her lab above the shop, sensing currents, drafting ideas, and transcribing these onto paper patterns and cotton calico models. She would alter and refine incessantly until, after one or two months, the final item would be cut out of selected cloth or leather. The cycle for each season always followed the same route. It began with research, drawing, experimentation, and prototyping ending with production and a fashion show. For my mother, the ultimate moment of public transferral, including the display of the collection on the shop floor and the staging of a catwalk, was superseded by depression and the start of the next phase of research and experimentation.[48]

The *DELISS* houses on Beauchamp Place were active laboratories for design and production. They incorporated not only the architecture of the buildings with their domestic living rooms and landings, but also the distinct competence available to dressmaking and fashion design at the time. Arriving at the Weltkulturen Museum in 2010, I recall feeling as if I had entered a *maison*, not unlike John Galliano, or later Raf Simons, when they first took over Dior. Extensive collections of rare materials and historic designs displayed remarkable ingenuity and craft. But here too, as in traditional haute-couture, in-house skills and expertise had remained the same for decades, with changes made only in absolute moderation.

The Weltkulturen Museum was full of ingenious ideas on how to best stock the collection. In the eighties, one conservator had come up with a couple of inspired proposals for storing numerous objects of one kind. These included various wooden clubs from the African continent usually built from a thick baton topped with a bulbous carved head. To stack them in an orderly manner, he constructed a long narrow shelf perforated with holes. Each club was provided with a small paper funnel to protect the neck of its shaft and placed vertically into one of the cavities. The result was both efficient and incongruous. This line-up of assault weapons with their paper cones reminded me of inverted prosciutto hams, only without the fat drips. Another invention was tailored to stack 1,500 swords, daggers, knives, and arrows that formed part of the 10,000 weapons in the museum's possession. With the common sense of a carpenter, the same conservator had hinged a series of plain wooden doors to the wall and fitted these with small leather straps. Once fastened into place, the form of each weapon was contoured in green or black felt-tip pen. Were an item to be removed, its outline would immediately indicate its correct placement. In 2013, for the show *Foreign Exchange (or the stories you wouldn't tell a stranger)*, we unscrewed the group of twenty doors holding hundreds of knives and daggers, and fixed them onto the wall of the exhibition space. It took more than two weeks to unpack all the weapons and return them to their appropriate locations, thereby testing the efficiency of the original design. And, for the first time, we needed to install a sensor in the exhibition just in case an overzealous visitor attempted to remove an arrow or a knife.

Our bricoleur even found a solution to storing Aboriginal paintings. Fragile and often decorated on both sides of a sheet of fine bark wood that was frequently warped or splintered, he had come up with a system of portable encasements. Boxed within a wide wood frame with panes of glass on either side, each bark painting was wedged into polystyrene. To complete the picture, the conservator had simply extended the outline of the bark by drawing directly onto the polymer clamshell. This DIY vitrine demonstrated an intelligent combination of makeshift aesthetics and functionality. His designs addressed not only questions of conservation but also the requirements of a research collection: artifacts needed to be made available for periods of observation and analysis that went beyond the opening and closing of a drawer.

There was no furniture for the kind of laboratory that I wanted to set up. So, I invited the Viennese designer Mathis Esterhazy to produce an overall plan for furniture structures that might accommodate a variety of artifacts of different shapes, sizes, and materials. Known for his tailored collaborations with artists and architects, Esterhazy designed a modular system for all the museum's ergonomic needs, including the offices, workspaces, and exhibition rooms. He began by developing a series of interlocking units, beginning with an aluminum desk and a presentation shelf on wheels. These prototypes were made in Vienna and brought to Frankfurt for the museum curators and conservators to test; Esterhazy then refined the designs in response to their comments. The result was a set of multifunctional mobile tables and units with alternating heights that could be varied according to the artifact's shape. Handmade in Vienna, this furniture became the physical heart of the laboratory environment.

Without his designs, the possibility of displacing objects from the stores and setting them up in an experimental space would have been thwarted on the grounds that these priceless objects might be damaged. Yet it was logical to produce furniture for the specific needs of a new multidisciplinary research venue. No office supplies or home furnishing stores could have provided the technical efficiency for this form of collection-centric labor. What was needed was a combination of functionality and neutral aesthetics that not only suspended the inevitable anachronism so common to ethnographic displays but actually aided the circulation and analysis of these artifacts rather than their containment. By introducing the laboratory as an additional space of inquiry within the museum, the issue of access would be opened up wider than ever before, necessitating a lot more interaction.

If one model proved significant in the laboratory's planning process, it was the Schaulager in Basel, a venue spearheaded by art patron Maja Oeri and the private Emanuel Hoffmann Foundation.[49] When I visited the Schaulager in July 2010, it did not matter that the collection was not ethnographic but centered on contemporary art. Far more relevant was to ascertain how it functioned, and how much access was enabled to the artworks. It turned out that physically working in the rooms for longer periods of time was not feasible. There were no tables or chairs inside the artists' individual storage spaces, so that the average time of study stretched at the most to an hour and a half in the presence of a curator who stood nearby. The presentation of each artist's room was neither fish nor fowl, neither curated nor uncurated, and for this reason, it was extremely stimulating, working better with certain artists than with others depending on the nature of the works and whether they could be easily inspected.

The more I saw of the Schaulager, the more I began to think that it was a *post-operational* space unlike the *pre-operational* rooms of the new laboratory in Frankfurt. It presented artworks seen from the perspective of the collector and the artist: produced, transacted, and evaluated. In contrast, the so-called ethnographic collection was unauthored and incomplete, with meanings barely transported by the impartial interpretations of custodial ethnography. The pre-operational laboratory implied that the work of inquiry had not reached its peak and that whoever came to conduct research would be proposing tentative and critical representations that would operate concurrently with the urgency to remediate the undocumented provenance and absent biographies of these artifacts. Moreover, what actually signified the difference between the operations conducted in the lab in Frankfurt and those executed at the Schaulager in Basel was ultimately the issue of access. Guest artists, writers, and scientists who took on a residency at the Weltkulturen Museum were given the keys to the ground floor laboratory. There tables and shelves, designed and built by Esterhazy, provided a flexible surface upon which to place the constellations of artifacts selected by each guest. There were no curators looking over anyone's shoulder. On the contrary, it was clear to all that only trust and responsibility could generate new concepts and representations. Without this unmonitored access, the procedure of ideational encoding, based on alternative and potentially heretical dialogues with a collection, could not have taken place.

On average, it took one year to move from the first stage of research in the laboratory to the final exhibition. This recursive process covered a guest's first visits to the museum's stores, their selection of artifacts, books, documents, and photographs, their private inquiry in the laboratory, individual studio practice, and their public lecture toward the end of the residency. Through this decelerative relationship with the collection, we gradually apprehended and identified the theme and contents of a future exhibition. The guest artist's research and the prototype they produced directly influenced the forthcoming show's concept and parameters. As a result, those activities initially performed in the laboratory and not visible to the outside were subsequently transformed into collaborative parameters for public inquiry. By leaving some threads frayed and obviating the typical pat, hermetic presentation, I hoped that visitors would recognize an invitation to conduct their own fieldwork in the exhibition. However, this intentional inconclusiveness was not easy to legitimize against the guild of museum ethnographers with their honed, intransigent practice of contextualization and ostensive regional and thematic categories. Indeed, what I understood as giving space to the visitor by enabling them to engage in their personal research within the exhibition was construed as insufficient or even ignorant. Indeed, it is relatively rare for an exhibition to present the unfinished curatorial and artistic associations that have led to the final presentation and thus to display the subjective, labyrinthine routes and errors that concept work produces. Wayward notes and plans are removed and replaced with prosaic wall texts. For the 2018 exhibition *Hello World* at Hamburger Bahnhof–Museum für Gegenwart in Berlin, I presented the results of the *Dilijan Arts Observatory*, which I had organized in an abandoned electronics factory in Armenia in 2016.[50] Hanging on the wall were my notes, diagrams, transcriptions, and maps. In this sense, there is no standard moment when the exhibition begins to be operational and the curatorial process is over.

Museum collections are idiosyncratic composites. They reflect the egos of scientists and historians, the foibles of curators and artists, and the political desires of museum directors to compete for new gifts and rare acquisitions. In contrast, *research collections* are transitory, named only in relation to an inquiry. Lacking in recorded authorship, they remain outside the art market and are assembled in a museum, institute, or university because the paradigm of the moment suggests that one can learn something from them. As constellations of material artifacts or archival documents, we rely on their ability to support teaching and ignite further research at specific moments in time. However, this value is quickly superseded by any results they generate, as well as parallel transformations in the arts and sciences that may contribute to qualify their ongoing validity. If reanimated through contemporary heteroclite assemblages that deconstruct their initial, source-centric classifications, they can infer alternative narratives and interpretations that both collide and collude with one another, as if their reappraisal had the potential to spam the canon. As exercises in visual thinking, research collections play a generative role in transdisciplinary education and knowledge production. Their remediation—as exemplified by ethnographic collections—encourages conceptual liminality across modes of representation from science to art, from *paideia* to *poesis*, such that to hoard them is to handicap their energy as "epistemic objects" able to weave new nodes of contact into the texture of human relations.[51] Time's passing works to disenfranchise artifacts in research collections through the inadequacies of academic discourse, but also through gaps in documentation, incorrect histories and the multiple contradictions that emerge when things are concealed. For decades, the vast potential of ethnology's research collections has been ignored by its own discipline, relegated to the anachronistic scientism of past paradigms.

In his work on agency, Bruno Latour introduces the distinction between "ostensive" and "performative" definitions.[52] Applied to the condition of ethnological artifacts, Latour's proposition infers that the ostensive definition actually precedes the ethnographic, and thereby the process through which ethnographic exhibitions are developed. An object that is searched for in order to illustrate or represent a presupposed religious faith or a sociocultural context, or any other ethnological category, will not be altered by its own display. Contextualization is predetermined by selecting and presenting an item, which is to be read in a specific manner. In contrast, a performative definition suggests that the artifact in the collection can actually generate new, unexpected interpretations that are mutable, possibly incommensurable with one another, but by no means set in stone. This impermanency enables an artist, for example, to act from the perspective of the "mediator" rather than the "intermediary" of definitions.[53] The outside guest—external to the discourse of ethnology—produces additional conceptual optics or visual ideas that are likely to have nothing to do with the canons that both museum visitor and professional seek to maintain. Remediation, in the sense of Paul Rabinow's dialogical methodology of healing and transferring, is predicated on an extension of the (re)mediatory role. Rabinow writes:

> The challenge is to turn a collection of separate entities, however distinctive, into a dynamic site for experiencing and reflecting on our history, our future, and our uneasy and unsure mutual connectedness. We need to move from a vision of a world of separateness and hierarchy to one of multiplicity, creativity and worth beyond the exotic. Said another way, the "our" in our history, future and potential connectedness is what needs to be thought through, reinvented and presented in such a way that it matters for those who come to a museum of world cultures. Placing too

much emphasis on diversity and discreteness leads to a pale relativism with a complex if at times sordid history; placing too much emphasis on their commonality leads to a pale humanism with its own thinned out legacy. One way to navigate this slalom between the too particular and the too general is to turn the parceled collections into an assemblage, carefully wrought, and to produce a vision, open, detailed and precious of World Cultures. If that vision or presentation is open to change, conflicts of interpretation, creative re-invention then vitality, or at least its possibility, can be restored to these artifacts of lives once lived and collections collected.[54]

The distinction between intermediary and (re)mediator identifies the implicit friction between the anthropologist internal to the museum and the external guest. The common assumption is that the museum anthropologist's status of scientist can be pitted against the uninformed extrapolation of the artist whose lab work is aligned with vague notions of inspiration or, at best, artistic research. The expertise of museum ethnographers relies on owning the keys to context and thus the authoritative frame of the object in question. In this sense, their input is isomorphic with their output, like some self-perpetuating prophecy of ethnological eschatology. The knowledge they trade in finds its currency in the construction of authenticity projected by the museum ethnographer onto the unauthored exhibit.

In contrast, an artist who engages with the museum is likely to pinpoint other meridians within the corpus of the collection, walking down alternative corridors in the storage spaces, and asking for a ladder to inspect something placed well out of reach. This process dislodges the authority of expertise that the custodian holds onto. Penetrating the depot's confinement, the outside eye transgresses. It selects and calls out a response from the object, bringing it out, recollecting and reclassifying it through a heterodox dialogue of elucidation. In so doing, the exogamous person, who collects the collection anew, breathes presence back into the artifacts, restores consciousness to their unfinished status, and helps to heal the disposition of the institution. In turn, objects become agents, animating a new indexical relation to the phenomenon in question, revealing another side to their optics, forms, grammar, and position in history. The legally administrative hold on collections by a museum or a municipality cannot control the potential meanings and narratives generated by these artifacts.

Subsequently, there is a marked tension between the overflow of materiality within ethnographic collections, the omissive histories of these largely looted goods, their ongoing absence in locations of origin, the semantic effects of their complex movements across worlds, and the current neoliberal conditions that determine global cultural exchange, including the politics of restitution. Working in a museum-laboratory consists of capturing the surplus of meanings that emerges when processes of reconnaissance and identification are set in motion. Someone may pick up a bowl because they are looking for a material that had been incised in a particular way, but then this same bowl will allude to quite different coded meanings. By assembling new constellations, the artist as a (re)mediator of associations will encourage the object to perform an excess of translation, nourishing clashes and encouraging refusals and revelations rather than allowing the aesthetic and semantic dimensions to fall onto an overriding ostensive definition.[55] Faced with so much non-knowledge, agency goes viral in the ethnographic museum. It multiplies and propagates but also breeds resistance, generating controversies that confront the canonical.

Museum anthropology presents different disciplinary measures and explanatory methods in order to build a fenced paddock around what it imagines to be the unbroken, undisciplined, or feral. The model-builder is always authored in contrast to the object of desire. The colonial collections still held in numerous European vaults are signed by mass anonymity. They may represent a moment in European history, but today they urgently require care and attention. The decolonial process in art history today cannot be engineered without full access to these disenfranchised objects sequestered and fetishized by museum anthropology. Isolated, they have no author that has been identified, no attributed maker other than through the *nomos* of the grouping, caste, tribe, or nation of people, recorded and confirmed by the ethnographer, and to which they are designated to belong. Their intellectual property rights are obfuscated and even denied. Could such charged research collections, effectively booty from the gray zone of scientific anthropology, become the focus for a new space of Jacques Derrida's "critical resistance?"[56] Peter Osborne asks:

> What does a practice, whether artistic or not, need to do to one of these objects in order not to reinscribe it within the same ethnographic system from which it derives? ... One danger is simply that the collection becomes the artistic means for a new practice, so that the collection is just subjugated to the logic of contemporary practice. It's like a new resource, and it becomes instrumentalized in contemporary art. The other danger is that these new practices function only to reactivate the object in some way, and then disappear. If either of these happen, the relation won't work, and you won't create change.[57]

I realized then that it was I who factored dissent in the museum. I could not work within the majority position of museum ethnology but needed to carve out a new set of parameters for which singular, monocultural, and monodisciplinary knowledge production would no longer be an option. In a diary entry dated nine months after I started at the museum, I wrote, "I wish to consolidate the methodology that is emerging and being tested out in the laboratory, first by artists, designers, and now by writers. This curatorial condition in which guests are invited to do concept work in the museum has to be given support. But I also need to write about the conflict between old and new schools, between adherents, adepts, informants, and interlocutors. What currency do I employ? How do I define my exchange system here in Frankfurt?" Michael Oppitz encouraged me to pursue the model of fieldwork in the museum. "Yes," he said, "combine the work of a museum with the work of a university. To make anthropology into one thing again. That is, intellectual theory, fieldwork, and being with an object world, and not making this more disparate until you have art pieces that you exhibit in Dubai juxtaposed with the Mona Lisa! All this can be done if you take the basis of our field seriously, and that means doing fieldwork."[58]

In March 2010, I traveled with artist Antje Majewski to West Africa. Our journey was a spontaneous decision: I aimed to go to Dakar to dialogue with colleagues from the Laboratoire Agit-Art—in particular, the artist El Hadji Sy and the philosopher Issa Samb—before taking on my new role in Frankfurt. Majewski wished to return to Senegal to meet various people she had encountered earlier. She traveled with a large pink suitcase filled with artifacts that she had acquired on a previous journey to China. All these things had the same handheld size. But some were heavy and otherworldly, like a meteorite, and others were fragile and made from clay, shell, or vegetable root. She also took with her a large conch from Africa. Her action of bringing these objects to Dakar was curious for several reasons. On a superficial level, they contrasted with the mass of Asian merchandise imported into Senegal. Cheap Chinese commodities such as textiles and clothing, plastic household products and electronic equipment flood the markets in West Africa. The ideology of a short-span, low-cost response to the daily requirements of living is embedded in these ubiquitous goods. Yet here was an artist from Germany bringing examples of Chinese material culture to an African metropolis that did not feature in this wholesale souk of domestic appliances and factory-produced knick-knacks and remakes. The objects Majewski owned and transported across the seas in her personal luggage appeared as psychic carriers of the complexity of human relations. Their talismanic character transmitted both surprising banality and exoticism at once. Placed on the hotel table in Dakar, they appeared like an assemblage of objects trapped between the mundanity of everyday life and the intensity of symbolic projection.

This provided a second, more unusual provocation: Majewski was not looking to purchase authentic artifacts from Senegalese street markets to take back to Germany, but was overturning the routes of trade and communication by introducing six or seven foreign articles as conversation pieces. Her sessions in Dakar with Issa Samb and El Hadji Sy, which she recorded on video, were structured around a dialogical interpellation of these incongruous objects. Majewski's questions bracketed out the normative context to reveal an additional, latent language. In effect, what she undertook in her interviews was a form of reverse encoding, turning classifications inside out to expose the psyche of objects, the stored signs and memories that reside in their morphologies and their repeated invocation. In this sense, she was not far off from the tradition of German anthropology and its "Kulturkreis" method established by Leo Frobenius in the 1930s and later extended by Adolf Jensen. Seeking to map the existence of mythical practices across continents, they attempted to create affinities between technology, language and myth that would link the archaeology and aesthetics of distant sites to one another. Frobenius believed he had discovered an African counterpart to the imaginary Greek city of Atlantis at Ile-Ife in Nigeria. At the time, his cosmogenic approach to history stood in marked contrast to the pragmatism of British Functionalism, which emphasized fieldwork and individual participant observation as the key heuristic tools of social anthropology.

In many cases, twentieth-century developments in anthropology were characterized by the tension between a conception of objects as witnesses of *ethnos*, and the growing recognition of less stable conceptions of human agency and subjectivity. An ethnographic account could quickly resemble a psychiatric dossier or police interrogation with meanings produced through oral testimonials written down by the ethnographer who, like an analyst or detective, was encouraged to hold back on subjective responses and feelings. This tension generated moments in the history of the episteme when vagabonding anthropologists and ethno-poets wrote storylines full of travesties aimed to highlight misunderstandings—or indeed invent them—to create a crisis in colonial presuppositions of objective reportage. Critical self-reflexivity rightly haunts anthropology's penchant towards orthodox, positivist methodologies.

In the sixties, not long after Claude Lévi-Strauss had signaled a shift to the immaterial, a wave of experimentation took over debates in several African countries. With independence came an intensified exchange of ideas between the former colonizers and colonized intellectuals and artists, sometimes supported by outside agencies.[59] This led to an effervescence of new cultural initiatives. Artists, musicians, writers, psychiatrists, scientists, economists, and politicians traveled between continents, pan-African events mobilized energies, and practitioners activated a new aesthetics and politics of African nationalism by taking over former colonial buildings such as universities and art academies. Medical experiments with LSD and synthetic pharmaceuticals were carried out in numerous African countries, and the continent became a test-bed once again for new models extending from medicine to architecture.[60] South African therapist David Cooper, who worked with his Glaswegian colleague R. D. Laing, promoted anti-psychiatry sessions that involved listening to life narratives and searching for moments of radical dissatisfaction. In 1967, Cooper coordinated the Congress on the Dialectics of Liberation attended by Laing, Allen Ginsberg, Herbert Marcuse, and Stokely Carmichael from the Black Panthers. With Léopold Sédar Senghor, the new poet-president of Senegal, who was inaugurated in 1960, there was an unparalleled state investment of thirty-three percent into the cultural planning of independence. The Musée Dynamique—a geometric reduction of a classicist temple located on the corniche of the Senegalese capital—was inaugurated by André Malraux in 1966 with an exhibition of archaeology from Senegal and Mali. Across the road, at the heart of Dakar's large university campus, stood the neurological hospital Fann, which neighbored the laboratories of Senegalese historian Cheikh Anta Diop, who had pioneered carbon-dating methods.

I first heard about the Fann Hospital in the early nineties, when I started working closely with the Laboratoire Agit-Art. I was told how members of this artists' collective had been involved in therapy sessions and workshops. The crossover between painting, performance, and experimental psychiatry was an active element in the development of their work as painters, actors, writers, and philosophers. According to El Hadji Sy, the sessions they participated in bore titles such as "The Teaching of Deviance," or "Premature Deviation and Loss of Consciousness." Only a few years earlier, in the seventies, the German writer Hubert Fichte traveled to Dakar to interview Henri Collomb, Fann's first director, as well as African neurologists and psychiatrists who worked there, including Dr. Momar Guèye, who still runs it today. In Fichte's *Psyche*, Collomb describes the hospital in Dakar:

> Fann is ... a hospital that cares for those people who cannot be helped by the usual methods. These are individuals that we describe as existing in a state of transculturation .... We use classic anti-psychotic drugs up to a point. But mainly patients are treated here without electroshock treatment or anti-psychotic drugs. We use a kind of group therapy, an ambient therapy (*thérapie d'ambience*) .... However, sometimes electroshock treatment satisfies the desire for an initiatory death, like a symbolic death, something that in traditional African societies precedes every new phase of transformation or development, and that can take place at the start of a psychiatric illness as much as it can signify the healing of it.[61]

The curative is the red thread between the alternative therapies at Fann and the metaphysical dramaturgy of the Laboratoire Agit-Art. Issa Samb's courtyard in Dakar's city center, which was decimated upon his death in 2017, was not merely a cemetery for discarded performance materials. Instead, each of the minor objects Samb cared for was inhabited by an extended relationship to the living, which he activated nearly imperceptibly as he altered their placement on a daily basis. Through his actions, the static, commemorative understanding of the museum as a holding or store was dissolved into the fluid agency of objects. For, as Samb liked to repeat, "Each time an individual moves an object from one place to another, they participate in the changing of the world. Who is to tell us that the leaf that falls from the tree is not our sister?" he asked. "An object is charged with history, with the culture that produced it originally and, as such, it is a constructed object." "Objects do speak," he continued, "but they speak their own language. Like the wind speaks. Like birds speak."[62] As he sought to show in his philosophical actions, which were never intended to be captured and transacted as art works, such technofossils of human ingenuity have an apposite hold over time. They affect our environment in such a manner that to remediate them by introducing them into a foreign context is to unexpectedly heal the scars of history. His methodology contradicted the ethnographic museum's focus on permanence and preservation. The tattered stained fragments of cloth dangling on frames and the weathered oxidized metals and washed-out photographs contravened any notion of museological conservation and suggested a defiance of the market—of either being purchased as single artworks or recouped as part of an ethnographic collection. These anomalous artifacts were part of a wider web of interdisciplinary inquiry and were not the production of just one person, but the result of a dialogue between many members of the collective.

Throughout the 1990s until his death in 2017, the incongruent character of this yard, hidden behind an unassuming entrance in Dakar's busy city center, suggested something of an alchemical laboratory. Between the scattered matter, seemingly caught in a *caput mortuum* phase of degeneration, one could read quotations, aphorisms, and traces of experimentation in chalk and charcoal script on black and on white boards. A long table surrounded by chairs bore witness to daily meetings and impromptu sessions. Pamphlets and invitation cards, reminding one to attend diplomatic cocktails, literary readings, or exhibition openings, lay piled together with notes scribbled on small pieces of paper by people who had passed by. All this created an impression of choreographed chaos. I read in this scenario a deviant language of philological interpretation not dissimilar to the base materialism that Georges Bataille had evoked in his journal *Documents*.[63] In the entry for *poussière* (dust),[64] he acerbically points to the philosophical ramifications of rituals of domestic cleanliness that speak against impending death and the gradual decay of matter over time. To illustrate his text, he chose two photographs taken in a storage space of the Musée d'Ethnographie du Trocadéro in Paris, which feature several naked mannequins and various ethnographic artifacts, all covered in debris and dust. My experience in Dakar, most powerful between 1992 and 2002, was an education in itself, an initiation into the Laboratoire Agit-Art's methodology. I cared for this dialogue and in publishing the first pilot issue of *Metronome* in Dakar, I positioned my practice between debates. To be consciously splayed between sites, discourses, and methodologies also rendered my position vulnerable. I chose then and as I do now to confront the animosity and exclusionary tactics that accompany expressions of professional territorialism.

Over the years my practice has consciously played with the transgression of roles, narrative forms, and institutional contexts in art. I studied contemporary art, then social anthropology, became an independent curator and researcher, and then a publisher. I moved incessantly to different cities to live, work, and print. *Metronome* was one outcome of this transitional modus operandi: a publishing organ that I initiated in 1996 in Dakar as a collective artwork and a curatorial methodology.[65] Through *Metronome* I could practice a form of direct and autonomous collaboration with artists, free from the constraints of museum curating or exhibition making increasingly aimed at large audiences. Too backstage for museums to finance, I sought support from foundations, educational institutions, and private individuals, and secured my own survival through contracts with art colleges, taking up artists' residencies, and moving from London to set up base for six months or more in Dakar, Berlin, Basel, Vienna, Frankfurt, Oslo, Stockholm, and Tokyo. *Metronome* was subjective and under the counter. Artists had to trust me to produce relevant arteries of ideational and visual flow out of their semi-formulated research ideas, which included drawings, plans, photography, scenes of action, manifestos, and fiction. It was a curatorial conduit in print form aimed to short-circuit communication between artists who coexisted in time yet worked in different locations with varying economic, spatial, and digital divides. I published unfinished works in written or visual form that were porous enough to incite professional curiosity in as yet unidentified colleagues.

I named this dialogical condition the *prelusive* phase, basing it on the proposition that a part of aesthetic knowledge can be transmitted before it is made public or exhibited. I see the prelusive phase as free-ranging and uncontrollable, yet able to transport the feverish state that drives both artists and anthropologists into areas of intellectual and corporeal disjuncture, testing their capacity to articulate the emergent, incomplete stages of their inquiries. Such intersubjective conceptualization corresponds to my understanding of fieldwork but is rarely identified in ethnographic reports or exhibitions.[66] In its idiosyncratic and analogue manner, *Metronome* publications brought artists across the world into contact with one another without the need for explanatory contextual information. What emerged through *Metronome* was the editorial trace of our conceptual intimacy. For this reason, it was more often compared to an artwork than a publication, and in this respect it contradicted the presupposition of descriptive objectivity in ethnography.[67]

I called *Metronome* an organ because it was generative and fragile. Each issue was contingent on my ability to mobilize contributions that I would encode according to the graphic design of earlier organs that had been published by individuals or collectives. Whenever I was invited to produce an issue, I began by searching on site for an earlier periodical that had once manifested the needs of artists and writers to declare their stances. There was no editorial team or regulated time structure. I even designed my own system of names and numbers for the total of seventeen publications. All these were ruses, which I deployed to aggravate the focus and articulation of *Metronome*'s circulation. For *Metronome* No. 3 "Tempolabor," I poached the layout of a specific edition of *Justine* by the Marquis de Sade published by Jean-Jacques Pauvert in 1968 with a preface by Georges Bataille. The graphic design, size, and binding of *Metronome* No.3 was a loyal copy of this earlier publication, and its contents corresponded accordingly to an act of mimetic appropriation. Slitting each page open with a knife, the reader would be drawn into the dramaturgical transcription, a meeting that took place behind closed doors, which I curated for the Kunsthalle Basel in 1998. Artists, activists, curators, and gallerists were invited to discuss the enigmas and dilemmas they faced in different art situations worldwide. Rather than produce a reader, with its sanitized, explanatory structure, I chose to work with the tropes of mid-eighteenth-century libertine literature and disguise the political potential of this *bureau d'esprit* by turning the transcription into a play with scenes and asides. I had no need for a graphic designer, only the craft of the typesetter, who would translocate all the stylistic elements of the original onto *Metronome*. A dictum that I carry with me and which originates from *Le Sopha* (*The Sofa*), a novel published in 1742 by Claude Prosper Jolyot de Crébillon, encapsulates the process in one line: "To know exactly where to stop short is perhaps harder than to invent."[68]

Metronome No. 9, which I produced in Paris with curator Thomas Boutoux, adopted the graphic layout of *The Stripteaser*, a neat promotional pocketbook of sixty-odd pages printed by underworld publisher Maurice Girodias at night to beat the censorship police. In the 1950s, Girodias's publishing house, Olympia Press, offered young French literati, international Beat poets, and friends of the penumbra a performative adjacency between life and work. By adopting this historical organ, I wanted to test the vitality of the debates fifty years on, and put a question to artists: what would lead you to withhold your authorship, remove your name, or use a pseudonym? Forms of communicational abstinence have always interested me, and this question related more to the artist's model of self-identification than it did to issues of censorship. With its eroticized choreography, the original *Stripteaser* accompanied the reader through sequences of women getting undressed followed by pages of short texts by Alexander Trocchi, Jean Genet, and William S. Burroughs, all in authorial disguise. According to the success of the tease, the reader could then locate the book they wished to purchase from Olympia Press.

With this prototype in hand, I was able to ask artists and writers in 2003 whether they felt the desire or necessity to withhold their name, and why? Liam Gillick, Tom McCarthy, Michael Archer, and Ina Blom transitioned respectively into Nancy Strasbourg, Susannah Mabbitt, Bella Woodfield and Bill Moan. Bjarne Melgaard, one of the seven guest artists invited to define a visual section, handed me a stack of color snapshots taken in a flat he had occupied at the start of the new millennium.

Calling it "Adresse Anonyme," he sought to redefine the locus of art by renting an apartment and living, performing, and documenting the extreme corporeality of a definition of anonymity. I collated the series and, as always, replicated the original graphic design of the prototype organ. For the launch, Boutoux and I hired all the rooms and the lobby of a typical old-style three-star hotel near l'Opéra in Paris and handed the keys over to the artists and their friends for twenty-four hours. Finally, in Tokyo, for an exhibition I had at Masato Nakamura's gallery Command N/Kandada in 2007, I produced an edition of sandals, which I made from second-hand books. I picked them up around Kanda district in Tokyo and they included a nineteenth-century illustrated bible, a cookbook, an atlas of the world, a biography of Sigmund Freud, Japanese technical dictionaries, soft-spine Manga comics, and several cheap thick French novels. I used these books to make flip-flops by returning to a printer and punching holes in the mass of pages through which I passed a knot of thick cord. A hardback provided a longer-lasting sole. A pocketbook indicated the size of a child's sandal. Every visitor to a Japanese home could tear off the worn page and enjoy a clean slipper, as well as read anew. This *Metronome* edition was called "Think with Your Feet" and while it referenced a line from Jacques Derrida, it bore no kinship to an earlier graphic design. It was a metabolic object.

After eleven years, I ceased publishing *Metronome*. By 2007, the Internet had become ubiquitous, offering default dissemination between artists, whose participation in the litter of biennials appeared to resolve the problem of how to identify a trusted interlocutor within the global field. Now everything had to be visible to be apprehended as contemporary art. With the lights on permanently, even the nocturnal mythic fell prey to the potency of illumination. Public visibility was the new drug pulling artists into event-led economic dependency. As a curatorial platform, *Metronome* appeared to have become redundant. Moreover, it merged into another, parallel project that I began running in 2001 and which impacted on my direction of the Weltkulturen Museum in Frankfurt. This was *Future Academy*, which I worked on for seven years in the UK, Senegal, India, Japan, the US, and Australia.[69] I wanted to know how the art college might mutate in the future, given the inflation of government-backed creative industries at the turn of the millennium. At each location, I mobilized self-elected groups of students in art, architecture, and science who speculated together on architectural, structural, and epistemological concepts for a future independent art institute. As with *Metronome* I moved to each location for longer periods, adapting my research accordingly, and finding support to nurture the project under the umbrella of local institutions.

In 2001, following the production in Scandinavia of *Metronome*'s "The Bastard" issue, I returned to London for family reasons and began working with Chelsea College of Art and Design. The London Institute (known today as the University of the Arts) had just bought the former Royal Army Medical College (RAMC) in order to rehouse the Chelsea College of Art and Design. This Victorian bastion built to educate medical doctors for urgencies in war was located on Millbank, next to Tate Britain. The top floors still stank with the putrid odor of dormitories. Other highlights included a spacious morgue, an operating theater, and cubicles in the cellar for testing responses to extreme heat and cold. Next to the disused operating theater, I discovered an organ library. Rows of empty shelves were labeled with black-and-white plastic strips that read "male genitalia," "intestines," "liver," and "heart." As part of their education, medical students in the late nineteenth century would thrust their hands into glass jars filled with the cold, viscous parts of a human being. Groping around, they sought to identify anatomies and remedies. Sensory information had to be immediately encoded into directives that might repair and potentially save an injured soldier at war in the colonies. There was no time to flip open a medical encyclopedia or phone home. This was the residue of a macabre archive for traumatic response.

Colin Cina, the outgoing dean at Chelsea offered me the vast space of the RAMC a year before the architects came in to transform it into a new branch of London's University of the Arts. He said, "Go and pitch your project to former postgraduate students in fine art and see if they want to work with you. If they do, you can have the whole building for nine months and develop a project there." They did, and having set up our headquarters in the Officers' Mess, a group of us met regularly to exchange our research on the history of the building. We focused on amateur dramatics, and the relationship between comedy and wartime conflict, eventually producing and printing *Metronome* 8A and 8B, "The Stunt" and "The Queel," as an edition with a two-page theater brochure printed on honey-colored and blue paper, somewhat resembling a man's corduroy coat and shirt, and an additional book in gray that looked more like a prison report. We held a twenty-four-hour public launch at the RAMC with guest speakers including John Latham, Cerith Wyn Evans, Michael Archer, and Catherine David, as well as film screenings, concerts, and a goulash bistro.

Similar to the museum, the legacies of nineteenth and twentieth-century art education need to take into account the colonial exportation of academic structures to Africa and India, for example.[70] And just as museums in 2020 wish for global diversity, art colleges too can no longer retain a purely localized approach to what is taught, nor to the staff employed and competence they represent. The growth in heterogeneity since the millennium is unprecedented in the history of cultural and educational institutions. Which is why we need to return to research collections and locate potential artifacts whose agency cannot be contained and sealed off, but instead becomes inherently connected to moving and adaptive life practices. Perhaps one can begin to work with the ecological ramifications of a creolized exquisite corpse—producing an infrastructure that enunciates a new methodology of dialogical research capable of generating *organs of virtue*. Such objects and practices carry the potential to translate physical, mechanical and decidedly genderless concepts of power onto a condition of survival. The metabolic museum is about returning to the internal workings of art practice and sister forms of inquiry and locating a site that recognizes the ethics of producing non-visible, non-monetized, unforeseeable conditions. When Michel de Certeau speaks of reading as poaching, he seeks to disequilibriate the scriptural power of the written word and bring back those activities that have been sidelined to the informal, the everyday, and the disenfranchised. In his way, Allan Kaprow's "Un-Artist" also references the stored code contained within tangential activities that underwrite the artist's freedom to engage in signal scrambling.

Twenty years on, the "university without conditions" has not yet taken place. But in the art school, you can practically build a bomb and nobody will question it. And that loophole—that blind spot—in the expanding process of cultural and industrial normativity interests me.

Paul Rabinow, who visited the museum in the early days, encouraged me to experiment with collaborative methodologies, to develop form-giving exercises and connect objects to episodes within today's context. "Be vigilant and restive," he said. "Look at interferences and micro-practices… invent practices of knowledge production,"[71] and this was exactly what I hoped to do. Indeed, each guest I invited would transform and redefine our understanding of the laboratory. As we prepared it, I set up a series of public talks entitled *6000 Collectors*. The name came from a throwaway comment made by one of the custodians. It referenced the number of people who had contributed to the museum's collection. Maybe only 5,400 or 5,750 collectors were registered in the museum's annals, but that didn't matter. What counted was the need to shine light onto the trajectory of these artifacts and elucidate how they had entered the museum in the first place. Who were these six thousand-odd collectors? Were the majority from Germany? How many were professional anthropologists, colonial administrators, missionaries, or traders? How many were merely amateur enthusiasts? The Friends of the Museum was a club of just such lovers of the exotic, returning to Frankfurt from trips abroad with Nepalese jewelry, African sculptures, or Southeast Asian Ikat cloth. They were eager to have their cherished trinkets cared for and approved by the museum. Every ten days on average, another private person would call, hoping to offload their souvenirs and heirlooms. If accepted, the stuff would be quarantined, deep frozen for at least one week to kill off any living beings, in particular moth and beetle larvae. One gift could necessitate weeks of custodial labor from disinfestation to restoration, evaluation, and stock-taking. Interestingly, this inventory procedure was foreshortened by the custodians when it came to new works actually produced in the museum laboratory by guest artists and designers.

In 2013, PAM (Perks and Mini), the designer duo based in Melbourne and Paris, came to work with the museum for four weeks. After spending time in the reserves, they selected several items of clothing, which were brought to the laboratory for their analysis. However, the rules indicated that no hat could be placed on a head, bracelet on an arm, or trouser on legs for fear of compromising conservation regulations. I was informed that these rules were based on the preservation of artifacts for a minimum of 1,000 years. Even the smallest particles of skin would endanger their longevity. Artist Otobong Nkanga described this same rule from another perspective:

> When I was an artist in residence at the Weltkulturen Labor, I chose around 150 objects from the collection. The museum restorers do not allow one to have any direct contact with the objects because oils might stain and age them. So I had to work with special gloves. I began to think about the time when I worked at Sephora on the Champs-Elysées in Paris. We had to sell luxury products, so Sephora made us wear black gloves. I started to understand why: once you have a product and you place it on a black glove, you erase history. The object is presented against a neutral background and the client focuses only on what they see. It was interesting for me to think about what I had experienced as a salesperson, and then to introduce this idea to the situation here at the museum's laboratory.[72]

Flexible in spirit, PAM experimented with photomontage and produced a season's collection of clothing and accessories, which they generously donated to the museum. A year later, while walking through one of the depot's vast industrial floors, I pulled open a steel filing cabinet with the word *Labor* (laboratory) scrawled onto it in blue Biro. Inside I found their entire work: prototypes ranging from hats to dresses, jackets, shoes and even ceramic jewelry, all haphazardly piled together without care. What was going on, I asked? Why hadn't these gifts gone through the same meticulous classification and conservation procedures as all other donations or acquisitions that entered the collection? Somewhat curtly, I was informed that the transregional character of this work, which had evolved from PAM's heterogeneous assemblages, did not correspond to the museum staff's custodial responsibilities. Transgressing the geographical meant quite simply that no one was ready to take on the responsibility of cataloguing these creole productions. Furthermore, the authored status of the new works developed inside the museum questioned the authority of regional and ethnic subdivisions and therefore the classificatory regime of the museum. Had the keepers initiated this research, their selection would have followed a circumscribed path of referentiality and these historical artifacts with undocumented authorship would have retained their allocated custodial foster parent.

The controversy did not end there. When PAM took part in the exhibition *Trading Style* they chose to dress a shop mannequin in an outfit made both from their own designs and a number of items from the collection. "Walt," as we nicknamed him, wore PAM knitted socks, an early twentieth-century pair of embroidered indigo Sarouel trousers from Nigeria, a PAM bomber jacket with a distorted Coca-Cola motif, and a PAM baseball cap. Covering the dummy's head was a mask from Papua New Guinea collected in the early nineteen-sixties on one of the museum's typical bouts of serial kleptomania. PAM's unusual juxtaposition worked well but caused an outcry among the custodians who claimed that as a ritual object the mask needed to be properly contextualized and, if shown at all, placed in something resembling a reconstructed shrine. Visitors from Papua New Guinea, so it was claimed, would be horrified at PAM's installation. I replied that this assemblage represented a contemporaneous model of diasporic appropriation and hybridization common among the younger generation today, consciously crossing over ethnicities and cultural identities. For the first time, the Frankfurt museum attracted teenagers to one of its exhibitions.

At the end of each year, I had to submit the financial assessment of all the gifts made to the museum. This report included both citizens' endowments as well as original test works made by artists during their residencies and gifted to the museum. The latter varied widely and included an annotated chapter of Tom McCarthy's manuscript of *Satin Island*, a series of tall wood panels by artist Marc Camille Chaimowicz that he had stenciled with motifs derived from the artifacts he selected, and Nkanga's large schematic collage mapping out her research on currency, jewelry, and weapons. All the guest artists gave generously, helping the museum to build a new collection, which directly referenced the historical artifacts and the photographic archive. Thomas Bayrle donated the *Trap for Stupid Cars* that informed the weaving method for his large-scale work at Documenta 13; Antje Majewski offered a portrait of one of the prehistoric stones from Papua New Guinea; and Simon Popper gave the museum several large-scale renditions in gouache of sets and series of objects in the collection. The financial evaluation of these works raised complex and interesting questions. The city requested this assessment on a yearly basis. It was invaluable for insurance purposes, but also as an estimate of the total capital of each city museum in Germany. But how could one work this out?

Each guest received an honorarium of 4,000 euros for a four-week residency, which in 2010 was a fair fee. In addition, there was a materials budget that varied between 1,000 and 2,000 euros. This was necessarily modest. I did not want to place pressure on artists or writers to perform during a mere monthlong residency. Further, with its municipal funding, the museum could not have afforded high-end productions. Instead, I hoped that the laboratory situation would stimulate critical and conceptual work based on individual research into the collection. If the experiment was successful and something emerged from this inquiry, then the guest was asked to leave a trace behind, thereby augmenting the existing ethnological interpretations allocated to the historical artifacts. I also hoped that this ideational environment would generate developments in their work once our collaboration was over. But how to place a figure on their experiments? Did one set up a hierarchy of value based on which gallery they belonged to? Should one simply multiply the residency fee? By how much? On what grounds? How did the friendships created at the museum, as well as the transdisciplinary professional dialogues between artists and regional custodians, impact on how we evaluated what was produced on site? In what manner did the new works made during laboratory residencies relate to the financial evaluation of the historical objects they had selected? An anonymous fish trap was no longer just an item collected during the Sepik expeditions of the nineteen-sixties, but something identified by artist Thomas Bayrle. Did this relation feature on the inventory card? Did we need to alter the insurance value of the fish trap too?

What began as an engaging braintwister acquired serious ramifications as it began to throw light onto the unresolved and often arbitrary assessment of collections of ethnographica harbored by so many museums in Germany. I recall a moment when one object was lost during a workshop at the museum. It was a small mouth harp. I was informed that it had an insurance value of one euro. Other objects considered to be masterpieces might graduate to several thousand, but once again, evaluation was a rough and ready process carried out by the custodians on the basis of a few auction catalogues and dealers' estimates. The travesty of this naïve capitalization of financial worth by a municipal museum in Germany might eventually flip back onto questions of restitution and even of resales. Restitution was rarely discussed in the museum and only one return took place during my tenure. It concerned a "Toi Moko," a Maori head, one of several held by Frankfurt's museums.

Against the dinner-party conversations on the pros and cons of restitution, archives with or without documented authorship are still being sought out, bought out, and impounded by museums, foundations, and mega-galleries in the name of conservation. Sacred forests in Cameroon are being hoovered up by avid museum anthropologists and hospital-quality MRI scanners are deployed to analyze the remains of rituals and investigate the inner tracts of sacrosanct sculptures. Revelations produced without consultation or participation from the holders of this initiate knowledge are obscene, neo-physiognomic articulations of academic authority based on the inalienability of ownership. To adulterate the currency of today's archive mania is no simple task. As with organ trafficking, acquisitions concluded on the US and European so-called tribal art markets, are driven by a coterie that plays on the blind eye of partisan states and the manipulation of legal parameters by curators, academics, auction houses and galleries. With practically no deaccessioning of collections taking place in European civic or state museums of ethnology, it is a complex undertaking to evaluate these artifacts let alone insert them within a legitimate market. While it appears extreme to compare the international organ trade with this branch of the global art market, the necropolitical binds both the symbolic, existential and economic dimensions of these infrastructures. There is no convincing argument for the retention of so many hundreds of thousands of artifacts, often collected in duplicate numbers, in ethnographic museums.

A Museum in Reverse

Over the course of the twentieth century, a process of aesthetic and semantic devaluation has taken place in the majority of European ethnographic museums. Gradually these invaluable historical holdings have receded into the shadow of contemporary knowledge production. Today, they capture our attention once more, but for other reasons: through legitimate and politically charged demands for restitution to their countries and cultures of origin. What does it mean to experiment with collections that have been embargoed within institutional frameworks directly founded on historical and legislative relations to colonialism? Is critical and creative remediation even possible? Can one heal the past with contemporary interpretations of these artifacts and are these new meanings powerful enough to implode the normativity of ethnographic identifications? Is there a model of institution today that dares to confront the sheer material enormity of the world's aesthetic production? For the millions of singular artifacts now held in European museums there are no makers that have been recorded by name other than in reference to the generic groupings of people to whom they are presumed—by anthropologists—to have originated from. Rather than reaffirm the dominant culturalist link between objects and *ethnos*, a post-ethnographic institution opens its doors to a scholarship that experiments with new criteria of evaluation based on a contemporary engagement with these research collections from the past. Culturally heterodox, such a structure has to be inclusive of transdisciplinary practices that have as yet no museological home. Taught around the globe, they include different formulations of postcolonial, cultural, and curatorial studies, product design, and contemporary art. As James Clifford writes, "No sovereign method is available, only experiments working outside the frozen alternatives of local and global, structure and process, macro and micro, material and cultural."[73]

Restitution has become both the central bone of contention and the most effective commodity to characterize the future of ethnological museums. Each of these maculate museums seeks the stamp of approval that comes with outing one's colonial collections by admitting to the blatant absence of solid written and photographic documentation. As a result of public lobbying and academic concern, and just as a generation of custodians is about to enter retirement, museum anthropology is experiencing a renaissance. The irony is that this renewed verve goes back to the source in order to recreate missing pieces of information omitted at the time of acquisition. All this is performed under the guise of object biographies and provenance studies. Arguments for and against restitution abound, but while these initiatives are addressed, ways of working with these vast collections retained in the vaults of museums in Europe need to be worked on. How can one engage in a revision of these collections in the twenty-first century? Why do these ethnographic holdings remain shrouded in invisibility? What might such a decolonial process entail in practical terms? What is stopping former European colonizers from providing space and access for students and researchers from the world's many cultures including indigenous producers, to study their heritage? What is the hurdle that blocks this process? Conservation? Toxicity? A deep-seated notion of ownership? Should legal leverage for rights of access be left to the unwieldy politics of repatriation and the underrepresented efforts of indigenous communities? When will architects consider the challenge of transforming repositories from nothing short of object-prisons to new spatial environments for experimental inquiry, for creating what I name the Museum-University? This hybrid proto-institution can make formal and informal university-level inquiry flow into former ethnographic museums, basing all new research on the potentiality created by assemblages of artifacts, documents, and photographic archives.

Michael Oppitz described the situation in 2011:

> Objects sit silently in repositories, the information about them lies asleep in the archives. They have to be opened up—with cosmopolitan flair and with money to support the researchers who want to work in the bowels of the museum. And this includes descendants of the societies that were robbed of these objects, or that sold them. It's a dialogic mission: invite people who can reconnect with the artifacts made by their ancestors through their own interpretations of them. It may help to ease the loss. And an important step into this future is the act of setting up a laboratory, as you have done, invigorating your place of work. In my view, it's absolutely right, and necessary. The Weltkulturen Museum is the only place in Germany where anything of that sort is happening.[74]

In 2013, I invited novelist Tom McCarthy to the museum, where he could feed his interest in "memory chambers and oblivion cellars" and draft *Satin Island*.[75] His key protagonist "U" is the in-house ethnographer of a media consultancy firm. "What do I do? I am an anthropologist. Structures of kinship; systems of exchange, barter and gift; symbolic operations lurking on the flip side of the habitual and the banal; identifying these, prying them out and holding them up, kicking and wriggling, to the light—that's my racket."[76] Using a double mirror of sorts, McCarthy not only wrote in the museum, but depicted this experience by merging the characters of some of the museum staff with my persona. The schizophrenia of his portrait of "Claudia" was palpable and when we exhibited his manuscript with a chunk of natural latex he selected from the Africa stores it caused another small outrage. This "lump of some black substance, all unformed" signified the base materiality of a diseased tumor and evoked the museum's metabolism as well as the book's subject matter. McCarthy had "unpicked" the "fiber"[77] of the institution's inner culture to expose not only the "whimsy dossiers"[78] but the small, obsessive, and recurring acts that defined the microdetail of its daily endeavor. In his shorthand, written during the residency, he remarked, "there are objects without documentation and vice versa—in the filing system, every document is duplicated/photocopied—they're trying to move everything over onto a database, digitizing it all—but in fact it's full of errors—so the database becomes just another form of narrative/story/fiction." He likened the storage bunker of the museum to a "giant sarcophagi" full of inner secrets. At one point, "U," the corporate anthropologist, is challenged by the custodian:

> What do you think, for example, she asked, opening another cabinet and pulling out a strange wicker contraption, this thing is for? A snow-shoe? I suggested. U., she said, it's from the tropics. Then a fishing net, I tried again. Maybe, she said. A fishing net; a ceremonial head-gear; a bat for playing some kind of game; a cooking implement ... Who knows? We don't. We won't. We haven't even catalogued half of this stuff. What should we do with it? Why not return it? I asked. That doesn't work, she answered curtly. The tribe's descendants don't know what this wicker thing is for either; they've all got mobile phones and drink Coke. And besides, if you repatriate an object it just turns up on the market six months later – may as well just send it straight to the collector's Texas ranch. That's even worse than us having it. So, they pile up here. [79]

Resident artist Luke Willis Thompson described the museum's collection as a mass of "objects in crisis that have witnessed the humiliation of ethnography."[80] To prepare his work in the laboratory, he asked the research curators to find "anything made from bone; anything used in sleeping; anything used in marking monuments, graves or events; anything that represents a person or a profession; any object that helps a body negotiate space; conversely any object that holds a body, binds it and shackles it; and any object that rejects trauma as a point of contact. In short, objects that have been in close proximity to a human body." His assemblages in the laboratory included shamanic chains made from one carved bone, steel slave shackles, a crib woven from thorns, and most significantly a headdress built from a human skull: an artifact high on the list of urgent repatriation. For a period in the mornings and evenings, Thompson sat down and stared at his grouping, in particular the decorated skull mask or "Lorr" from New Britain in Melanesia, which had been collected by Carl Gerlach in 1879. After three weeks, he handed me a page-long concept:

> My proposal to the exhibition Gift, Legacy, Acquisition, Exchange,[81] is to use my artist's fee to aid a family wishing to repatriate the body of a deceased member from Germany. The funding of this will ask for no direct reciprocity from the family, however the artwork will consist of a negotiation for documentation. The work is a conceptual response to the history of the museum and its shifting perceptions towards dislocation and relocation. The work is to operate with a question, if the existence of peoples was to be material evidenced through historical ethnography how can immaterial histories constitute (post, contemporary) ethnography today?
>
> Realization of the project: research will need to be made into pre-existing strategies for how communities negotiate the process of internment across national lines. The work will not seek to alter these strategies but to look at the various forms this takes and to document this where appropriate. This research will place us in connection with how families resource this process i.e. what financial aid is made available, or how and where self-resourcing is taking place. Where possible it may be useful to work with members of NGOs or community leaders. There are ethical problems with the work; however as a member of a source community who deals intimately with such a problem, there are also immense benefits for a gift of this kind. The most care will need to be taken around the offer of this funding, no application process would appropriate, and the simple selection of a family could be equally offensive.
>
> Outcome for gallery: The final outcome for the exhibition would be a collection of any documentation installed in the space in a minimal way, possibly consisting of readymade documents, images or moving image. The work would be

> accompanied by a short text explaining the gesture. All documentation would be installed with one artistic requirement, to be positioned on a wall on the axis towards mecca, if compatible with the belief system of the family.[82]

The work of the museum involved finding finding the appropriate person to pass on the artist's donation. With Yvette Mutumba, by then research curator for Africa, Thompson identified an imam who had created the first English-speaking mosque in Frankfurt and now ran an organization dedicated to helping Muslim migrants. After discussing the project at length, the imam agreed to act as the interlocutor between the artist, the museum, and a specific family who would receive the gift. Thompson explains, "I believe his willingness came from the fact that his twenty-two-year-old son passed away two months earlier. His son was a German citizen and for a whole host of reasons the young man had to be buried in Frankfurt against the wish of his family to bring him back to Egypt." The broker then instigated an essential shift in the artwork. He felt that asking the family for documentation of the deceased, as requested by the artist, might create difficulties around their acceptance of the donation. His suggestion was to separate whatever occurs in the gallery from whatever happens in the real world. "So we had an artwork that took on a bifurcation: the body and the money traveled in one direction, whereas objects that function as memorials traveled in another: towards the museum."[83]

Later, when Thompson's laboratory work was exhibited, it consisted of a certificate from the museum authorizing the imam to receive the gift on behalf of an anonymous person; a vitrine with the skull mask, slave shackles, and chain of bone. On the wall hung a series of amateur snapshots of the imam's deceased son.[84] This was not a "displaced repetition of the early modernist appropriation of these objects and their aestheticisation,"[85] but an experiment by Thompson to build a constellation that would be, as he states, "interdeterminate: neither sacred, nor authentic or inauthentic." Rather than ideologize the restitution of human remains, the artist had pointed to the here and now of dying in the international city of Frankfurt. He demonstrated the complexity of practices performed below the radar of mainstream cultural institutions, pointing to current procedures that combine economic, religious and ethical imperatives. His work critiqued the assumptions promoted by local politicians that the world cultures museum had the wherewithal to address marginalized communities either historical or contemporary. In this manner, Thompson formulated a "museum in reverse" built on dissemination and dispersal, on giving away rather than accumulating.

Conceived as a universalizing mission embedded within the utopia of cultural conquest, the ethnological museum was bound to remain incomplete. Yet the Enlightenment desire to create an all-encompassing encyclopedia of artifacts from every region of the globe persisted regardless of the impossibility of representing the world through its material culture. In Germany, the establishment of *ethno-colonial* museums in the mid-nineteenth century was closely entwined with anthropological methods with which to measure, compare, depict, identify, classify, and exhibit people as if they were goods. Collecting expeditions were systematic, organized endeavors that provided a foundation for sidelines in trade and strategies for long-term exploitation. Ethnographies were read as guidebooks by commercial entrepreneurs who needed to know whom they were dealing with, as well as with what. The geography of trade constituted the underpinnings of the ethnographic museum in Frankfurt.

In the twenty-first century, these museums remain an extension of the complex regime of colonial and neocolonial governance. The Musée du quai Branly—Jacques Chirac, the British Museum in London and the Humboldt Forum in Berlin are prime protagonists of the guardianship of a universalist imperialism, declaring their doors open to visitors from the so-called source communities.[86] Imagine if asylum seekers arriving in Europe were to apply for visas on the basis of significant and necessary engagement with their sequestered cultural and familial heritage? Would the legitimacy of their request be founded on their right to research and exploit all designs and derivatives that might potentially emerge from an investigation of this past ingenuity? The common assumption holds that the "visit" prescribes respectful observation but leaves unanswered the limits of remediation. Is this purely a case of healing without translocation and redesign, as the term implies? Is quasi-barring access tantamount to protecting the current owner from losing out on future property rights?

Notwithstanding the proliferation of postcolonial studies, ethnology's scientistic inferences continue to provide the dominant framing of these collections, closely regulating which artifacts are to be exhibited on whose world stage and how they should be named and identified. A form of psychological compensation, shot through with biases on class and education, is deployed through wall texts and visual designs, which contrast with the more exclusive exhibitions of artworks from ancient Egypt, Greece, or Rome. The scenographic and theatrical model deployed in ethnographic museums comes closer to the normative aesthetic of the Kaufhaus des Westens in Berlin, Selfridges in London, or Galeries Lafayette in Paris. In the nineteenth century, ethnographic museums were constructed concurrently with the development of colonial trade routes and the promotion of mass tourism. Even today, exhibitions in ethnographic museums are produced like shop displays and signify the continuity of the colonial emporium as a place of gloating and simulation. Here you find out how other people sleep, prepare food, build shelters, wear clothes, or perform rituals, all within what James Clifford once named the "ethnographic present." So, what happens to the uprooted artifact in a world of high velocity and information surfeit, as we know it?

One afternoon, a sixteen-year-old girl visited the Weltkulturen Museum with a group of other pupils as part of an educational program. I showed her a sculpture that I had located in our stores and placed on the landing outside my office. It was by the Ugandan artist Francis Nnaggenda and had been purchased by the museum in the eighties. I called it Miss Kampala. It was a massive work, brilliantly carved out of one piece of wood with elaborate hair braids and glaring headlight eyes that had been inserted into the sculpture. Miss Kampala had no arms. It was unclear to me whether this sculpture represented an amputee or not. Yet Nnaggenda had carved amputees before, for example his *War Victim* from 1980, the central sculpture that stood in the library of Makerere University in Kampala. I asked the schoolgirl if she knew where Kampala was. She said, no, had no idea at all. Then, quite suddenly, she spoke about how she recently found out about South Baghdad—not Iraq, not Baghdad, but specifically *South* Baghdad. I was alerted to the discrepancy between such contemporary identifications and the artifacts in the museum. She had scaled down global geography to a suburban context, linking her own life in Germany to a neighborhood in the Iraqi capital. How could I bridge the gap between these two contexts, I wondered? This was the challenge that we faced at the museum: knowing how to come to terms with the hiatus between the narratives of then and now, the different geopolitical and associative identities, and their relation to crises and war, epidemics, and anonymity? Moreover, how to do this with a collection that had been brutally extricated from its original referentiality? Miss Kampala signified something of an *ethnographic amputee*, an example of an object that was incomplete, whose associative quality had been partially erased by the passage of time. "Beneath the hermeneutic patina: one no longer knows what this piece of wood, whose example suddenly looms up, is good for and what it is worth," writes Jacques Derrida in *The Spectres of Marx*.[87] Or as Michael Taussig suggests, "Let us be in no hurry to reveal this secret, whose exposure would destroy it."[88]

Objects are like flytraps. We are lured by them, our imagination seduced by their patina and provenance. But, in practice, this fascination is short-lived and selective. Their spectral charge is contingent upon each new claim of authenticity expressed through a concept of origin understood as ownership. For pedigree to operate on a so-called ethnographic object, proprietorship akin to an archaeological stratification of legal rights based on possession, has to be named. And this naming is repeated and evoked again and again. As a result of such amplification, certain items acquire aura and provenance, while others fall into obscurity. They slide out of time and are quickly forgotten by curators and public alike. Like Paul Valéry's ambiguous object, they are thrown back into the sea, their doubtful materiality and absent authorship making them sink down to the opaque depths of anthropology's catacomb of human and material culture.[89] The "afterlife of property" evokes the painful remembrance of transcontinental slavery expressed by the ongoing incarceration of ethnological collections.[90] All these hundreds of thousands of objects held in inaccessible depots, under the Seine in Paris, or secreted in the urban periphery, that "prison house of radical difference and negativity,"[91] begin to resemble muted populations sealed off and incarcerated in the holds of ships built for the slave trade. That this status persists today is due to the large-scale excoriation of the original authorship of these objects and their ontological reinscription within the regime of anthropology. If there is one particularly pertinent crime from the past that bears ramifications for today's reevaluation of these artifacts, it is the eradication by museum anthropologists, missionaries, and collectors of the names of the original makers, those artists, designers, engineers, architects, and craftspeople who devised these formulations of ingenuity, virtue, and survival. To address this erasure is to steer against the dominant current of monodisciplinary inscription and reductionist strategies of ethnographic display that reconfirm sole custody of these sequestered collections. Narratives in museum ethnography continue to retain master-slave terminologies that concur with the language of seclusion and control, such as the "keeper," "custodian" and "conservator."[92] This reservoir of world heritage is maintained in the implicit belief that therein lies an ambivalent energy yet to be converted and exploited by its current owners. Why else would Europe's museums wish to retain so many millions of artifacts pitilessly extracted from their countries of origin?

Whether one is dealing with inanimate matter or immaterial imaginaries, the process of extraction in the field of art is remarkably close to the illegal safaris of organ hunters. Organs—understood as units of living matter subject to global monetization—cross the borderlines of institutions, of cultural ownership, of illegal economies, and of personal and state sovereignty. The human body is usurped, dismembered, and traded under the radar, circulating between the criminal world of traffickers, impoverished donors, sick recipients, and unscrupulous medical staff. Organs are acquired by coercion, deception, and fraudulently obtained consent. Persons can be kidnapped, sold, and killed for their organs. The organ broker recruits their donors from army barracks, bars, jails, unemployment offices, and shopping malls.

In his manifesto "The Trans Body is a Colony," Paul B. Preciado writes that the "trans body is to normative heterosexuality what Palestine is to the West: a colony whose extension and form is perpetuated only through violence. Cut here, paste there, take out those organs, replace them with others. The migrant loses the nation-state. The refugee loses the home. The trans person loses the body. They all cross the border. The border constitutes them. They live at the crossroads.... The trans body is a colony of disciplinary institutions, of the media, of the pharmaco-pornographic industry, of the market.... When each tree has been cut down and each mountain pierced, there will be nothing else to fuck. Then the earth becomes a garbage dump, a huge trans body opened out and dismembered. The corpses of colonizers will be buried with the trans organs that they stole from us. Only our imaginary organs cannot be buried. They will live forever. Our imaginary organs will become the warriors of the crossing."[93]

It comes as no surprise that arguments surrounding potential toxicity help to legitimize the suppression, or euphemistically expressed, the safeguarding of these artifacts, within the confines of the repository. Toxicity resides in traces of poisons formerly sprayed onto foreign objects on arrival in Europe. It also lies latent as microbiome, identified on fragments of human remains. From the layers of dried blood that build a Bamana boli sculpture from Mali, to evidence of sperm excreta in penis sheaths from Papua New Guinea, these examples drawn from ethnographic collections raise questions around biosecurity and the viral agency contained in these objects.[94] More than before, the ethnographic museum has become a paranoid site of retention and a space of risk, leading to increased stockpiling and elaborate lab testing. Since the viral crisis of 2020, fears of zoonotic contamination projected onto artworks made from human and animal remains are sure to become more prominent, sealing off access ever more efficiently.

Today, magnetic resonance imaging is performed on artifacts considered to be high in mystical and religious power. Feet-first, as if they represented a corpse, these sculptures are made to reveal their hidden anatomy. This biomedical inner journey has begun to indicate tracts within the wooden mass that were previously concealed from the uninitiated eye. Internal conduits between the sculpture's mouth, penis, and anus enable ritual offerings such as oils or other elements to be imbibed and digested to the point of expulsion. When placed in the sun, a figurine in wood may simulate anthropomorphic qualities by exuding what appears to be human sweat. These laboratory analyses may help to understand the material constitution of artifacts, providing useful information for conservation, but they also invade the spiritual sanctity of the ritual sculpture. New research that probes into the vitality of these objects merges the archaeological with the bio-ethnological. Today everything can be scanned, from humanoid mummies to the more evanescent remains of rituals. But who agrees to these diagnoses? How far are artists, priests, and healers involved in deciding if such analyses should be performed on their heritage, whose coded knowledge has been enacted for centuries by way of these iconic sculptures? Is this new biomedical research taking place in all European ethnographic museums, and what self-critical position does it generate if at all? The return to physiognomic analyses is a scientistic reformulation of anthropology's problematic past transferred today onto sequestered collections.

Like the organ trade, the necropolitical colonial museum survives off the control and regulation of the nerve centers of agency. It confers toxicity onto ambiguous objects, perversely poisoning the institution's metabolism and calling out for new systems of healing. A new tug of war is emerging today around the legitimacy of future interpretations, but are the remediators blood relations? Are they agnostics within anthropology? Are they traders in grafts and technicians of prosthetics, of counterfeits so devalued in the social sciences and the arts markets of Western Europe?

Nearing four years in post, my boss convened me to his office. "Are you running a hotel or a museum?" he shouted. "You've employed a chef! If the papers find out, the headlines will read SODOM AND GOMORRAH!" He was alluding to aspects of the museum's infrastructure that had changed since I took over. Exhibitions morphed out of the laboratory's activities, which were qualified less by a focus on thematic propositions than by the old-fashioned exercise of observation and visual thinking. Subsequently, certain priorities changed, too. The institution began to circulate with people who slept, ate, worked, conversed, and engaged in the critical reassessment of the museum's extensive archives. To make this happen required the implementation of care, but also conviviality. To host artists and writers-in-residence was to be attentive to their needs and desires. "Yes," I answered. We did indeed have a gastro-anthropologist: a Fulbright scholar who ran our successful evening school called *The World in a Spoon*. Sebastian Schellhaas held weekly seminars and cooking workshops on the crossovers between science and art, which he accompanied with temporary exhibits showing a wide selection of culinary utensils and other implements from the museum's collection. His excellent work drew a large audience and warranted the publication of a book with commissioned essays on the anthropology of nutrition.[95] From time to time, he would prepare meals in the kitchen of the laboratory villa. There were planning dinners for numerous international guests, artists, diplomats, and funders. Not only was the gastro-anthropologist's nourishment more individual and economical than any traiteur, his hands-on workshops for the public and his dinners in the salon of the villa connected anthropological inquiry to the visceral nature of political negotiation.

Regardless of name changes and expensive interior design, the visitors see only the cosmeticized epidermis of a complex organism battling to survive in the twenty-first century. The corpus of the collection and the framework that determines its present usage activates responses that vary from repulsion and fear, to mourning and confusion. Not knowing today what might have been recorded then, such as the name of the designer or artist and their rights of ownership, signifies an act of violent disenfranchisement and subjugation. Indeed, from the start of my directorship, the question of legitimacy to alter the museum's existing configuration was both directly and indirectly raised by the staff. From my third week in post, the human resources department had begun gathering rumors and misgivings on the changes I was initiating at the museum. The paradigm had been framed by the former directors, all German ethnographers, doctors, and missionaries. I was the ninth in its history, the first from outside the lodge, and the second in a row to be dismissed. The history of this museum's intransigence was known to the city, but there was little that could be done. My attempt to innovate this institution and reposition research into its collections through a methodology of external remediation was more than the city expected or desired. Ultimately, my case of unfair dismissal had nothing to do with administration, financial regulation, or staff discontent. It was a battle of method and meaning, resulting in friction between procedures of artistic research and the rules of ethnological museology.

Not long ago, I was asked what I thought about the future of the world cultures or ethnographic museum. I replied that it no longer exists. It cannot continue as it has for the past 150 years. The public function of this institution has to change to the core. For the worst scenario would be for these already malfunctioning presentations of peoples of the world to be instrumentalized for sinister, xenophobic intentions. If the ethnological museum no longer exists, it is because the scale of the colonial cultural endeavor is only slowly becoming visible to the world, triggering responses for which the juridical argument of restitution provides the greatest leverage for the right of access to these collections. The ethnological museum as a reservoir of energy, an "orgone accumulator"[96] of cultural consumption, still fired by colonial greed, no longer pumps enough energy into the system for it to survive unnoticed. The Humboldt Forum in Berlin has testified to this. Morgue to the destruction of peoples or memorial to the colonialist salvage of cultures, the damnation of memory is to identify that moment in time and then wish to preserve it and reclaim it. Slavoj Žižek speaks about statues as if they were immobilized human bodies, petrified *tableaux vivant* of human interaction.[97] Are occluded artifacts extensions of that idea, generated within a cryonic conceptualization of culture? But what if archives had the lifespan of certain houses made only of wood or rattan without deep concrete foundations to guarantee perennation? What if photographs and cloth held in collections were allowed to fade by being looked at and touched?[98] Could one begin to consider the sharing or co-ownership of historical artifacts across continental, political, and institutional agendas, enabling increased circulation, yet without a hegemony of art-historical canons to drive interpretations in a prescribed direction? What imperative might render ethnographic collections open-source and thereby dislodge the Eurocentric ideology of conservation? Is it possible to forge an internationally binding, legal resolution that obliges state and municipal museums to open up their depots and provide access to their holdings for several months each year? Might this help to dissolve the monocultural and monodisciplinary mix of fetishism and positivism that fuels these museums?

Between critical analyses of exhibition histories and various iterations of artistic research, curatorial practice today increasingly adopts a bookish frame for which artworks and artifacts are deployed as rhetorical exemplars within discursive and text-based methods of hermeneutical inquiry. The illustrational turn that characterizes certain exhibition formats today—be they intended for large audiences or more demanding peer groups—throws up a tension within the museological institution. At one end of the curatorial spectrum are speculative exhibitions that promote archival reconfigurations, proposing a new didacticism based on non-normative forms of contextualization. Here, as

Theodor Adorno once wrote, "art becomes a matter of education and information. Venus becomes a document."[99] At the other end is the generic art museum indicating a worrying return to its former colonial matrix, which like Adorno's "casino, cannot lose." This emporium of high-octane capital sells the global experience of art and luxury in the twenty first century, complimenting new estates and shopping malls with global brand outlets. The new museum—as Paul B. Preciado reminds us, is a "vector of urban gentrification, embodying the utopia of nineteenth century hygienism redoubled by the imperative of tourism. In this sense, a contemporary art museum in the neoliberal age is more like an airport than a library."[100]

Ann L. Stoler states that "colonial presence" is articulated through a "political grammar" that "occludes … hides and conceals, creates blockage, and closes off."[101] But what if there was intentionality behind a name undocumented rather like a willful act of retention designed to produce a form of communicational abstinence? Today the absence of the artist's name, be it violently excluded or intentionally withheld, throws turmoil into claims of ownership, patenting, and other forms of capitalization in artistic and aesthetic practices. The museum adapts quasi-automatically to its juridical features, economic imperatives, and performative articulation like a breathing, digesting, expelling, and restituting morphology of human interaction. Its internal metabolism is reliant on necessity, vitality, survival, and, of course, on desire. It cannot be afraid of intimacy. Yet energy flows that elicit constellations of aesthetic experiment and production also encounter organ failure. Indeed, chronic conditions in the institutional constitution of art and curatorial practice permeate our current models of thought and action. Artworks and curatorial projects easily become repetitive one-liners, pumping small shots of OxyContin into the art world's numbed and sprawling body. Young blood flows into twenty-first-century *salons pompiers* of art, but the biennial as an organ is redundant and has been for a long while. How to activate the required treatment, and with which *techne*, is the question faced today; *techne* here indicating the Greek term for craftsmanship and art, but also episteme and transmission.

The issue at stake is the sense of "vital relationships" that bring new understandings of cultural infrastructure to the museum.

How can one conceive of the conjunction of formalized knowledge production in exhibitions together with freestyle educational methods, which take over the normative architecture of a museum and initiate an autocuratorial mode on the part of the visitor? How can one generate a decolonial process in the teaching of art history and curatorial practice in order to emancipate students and encourage them to work in an ambitious way with collections and archives? What forms of temporary occupation and noncapitalized activity are possible in the museum of the twenty-first century? Could new formulations of higher education extend more aggressively across the museum, the art school, and the university? George Elder Davie claimed that "the most important side of any department of knowledge is the side on which it comes into contact with every other department."[102] For through the contrast medium of one institution in relation to another, one is likely to see beyond the "eddies of ignorance in epistemological space."[103]

To remediate the colonial museum requires a synesthetic process that engages not only with conditions of institutional blindness but equally with the architectural structures through which human beings are engaged in acts of sentient cognition with materialized histories from the past. The question is how to ascertain whether the ergonomic engineering of the human body in the parcours of the museum's architecture actually affects the scope and scale of hermeneutic unfolding? For example, is the entrenched polarity so often mooted between contextualizing exhibitions and aesthetic displays not predicated on the presence or absence of various *techne*, including pedestals, lighting, and wall texts? The focus on explanation as the lead ideology of so many museological displays holds back the visual dramaturgy of curatorial practice substituting it with a grammatical linearity of formalized knowledge production. Which other public environment pushes a person to stand and read for several minutes, often longer than the time spent looking at the artworks indicated in the narrative? The textualization of exhibitions replaces the (much criticized) retinal access to artworks and the broader corporeal and phenomenological apprehension of what takes place within the rooms of a museum. More specifically, these written elements vie for attention with the artworks, which may well include texts, too. Tracts on walls can be read as authoritarian methods to counterbalance any semantic snipers who, by introducing an oblique visual reading of the exhibit, risk annihilating the normativity that controls not only the art works but the bodies of the public. These are commands even if we prefer to read them as contextual background or introductions to the thesis behind an exhibition.

Today, there is growing recognition of the value of subjective historiographies drafted by artists on the basis of contested archives and collections. The engagement of artists demonstrates the desire to define a new malleable, heuristic space able to draw together different faculties, methodologies, and shifting social contexts into the museum of the twenty-first century. It indicates that an intersection between museum and university might help in the remediation of colonial collections thereby activating new forms of experimental visual inquiry.

"Where do we land today?" asks Bruno Latour.[104] Is this common space a local context, the land, the soil, *ethnos*, or a singular vision once again? Or do we need to work toward a multiplicity of critical zones and common places that take into account the plurality of organisms, of living beings, of various cultures and existences? If the museum is to provide its collections—and by extension artworks—with the oxygen necessary for their renewed emission and reception, it needs to take on the complexities of cognitive and emotional responses generated within its walls, opening up histories and their complaints to operations of curative inquiry. To reconsider the metabolic functions of the museum is to think about each of the organs that contributes to its overall institutional operations, subjecting collections to contemporary scrutiny and remediation. On the basis of new meanings and social innovations derived from their analysis, authors once excluded or undocumented by the procedural discourse of ethnology can be renamed, and intellectual property rights returned to their ancestors.

Wherever they are located, museums are urgently in need of a contemporary infrastructure to transition into a new architectonic venue for students and researchers from all over the world, a complex space where they can engage in multidisciplinary inquiry at university level based directly on the collections. These collections can be seen as reservoirs of memories waiting for emancipation,[105] as banks of stored code, as strata of symbolism, desire, and ingenuity and therefore as concentrates of energy whose economic value is suspended and whose circulation is hampered beyond the stores. To engage with such collections actually requires redefining the former imperial museum beyond its existing cursus toward a more radical understanding of intentionality. "New institutions," wrote Ivan Illich in 1971, "should be channels to which the learner would have access without credentials or pedigrees—public spaces in which peers and elders outside of his (sic) immediate horizon would become available."[106] Like Illich, Joseph Beuys also referred to the museum as needing a department of objects, which like a university would generate a "permanent conference on cultural issues."[107]

The first model of a Museum-University that I tested out post-Frankfurt took place in Kiev in advance of the biennial of 2015. This diary entry describes the modus operandi and the questions I raised at the time:

Museum-University Test 1

School of Remediation: A two-day micro-institution based on ergonomy and deceleration, at the National Museum of the History of Ukraine, Kyiv August 6–10, 2015.

Sitting together at the frontline of the museum around a table with a set of objects collected at the fleamarket the day before. The borderline of the museum. You've paid your entrance fee and you walk up the steps into the main hall. Before you can access the temporary exhibition, you find yourself watching and maybe participating in a seminar. This seminar is the first test of the Museum-University. A series of chairs denote a new department in the making. Three tables are placed together. A small pin board—hardly obtrusive—enables a few key words to be translated and presented: Museum-University/Welcome!/ Collage/Contested, Who is, or what is, the Outsider/the Outside of a Museum/Source Community/Tools/Work/Space/ Ergonomy/Specialist/Sociologist/Architect/3D/Archive/ Photos...

We send a signal out to the visitors who enter the museum. We invite them to sit down with us at the table, and several do. Some stay for the full four hours. An Italian economist, a man from Kyiv searching for an intellectual partnership, two very young women, hard to say if they are art students or not. The group is heterogeneous: artists, historians, linguists, students who do guided tours at the Pinchuk art center in town, members of staff from the history museum. We speak English. There are only a couple of people who can't speak it, and I can't understand any Ukrainian or Russian.

To set off the inquiry, I ask participants to go individually to the fleamarket in Petroska on Saturday morning. We are to search for *contentious* objects, artifacts that generate complex meanings, that operate on the edge of controversy or ambivalence, whatever their period or materiality. Each person works with a double desire: to collect something that fits the description and something they want to own. I obsess about finding a fur coat, like I'd need it in Berlin but also in Kyiv. By the end of the first day I know deep down that I want to negotiate a new situation with artists and intellectuals. The Museum-University is a first test, an experiment to see how thoughts move and bodies relate to museological space. In some ways the body issue is the most important.

Our collected objects include:

- one dinner plate with painted pansies
- four plastic shopping bags produced in the 1990s with various graphic designs and patterns
- two versions of cardboard files for placing documents (with name tags in Russian)
- one postman's bag made from thick canvas with a metal lock and handcuffs attached to the handle
- a set of six Bakelite cheese knives in an arc shaped holder
- three porcelain doll's limbs: two legs and an arm with a broken finger
- a thick rough fairly phallic piece of beeswax

- one red and black teapot commemorating Lenin's life (with dates of birth and death)
- one trolley symbolic of the first President Kravchuk and called a "Kravchuka"
- two T-shirts, on one: "Make Pierogi Not War," and on another two photographs of a family wearing sunglasses
- six drinking glasses from the Soviet period
- one small piece of lead placed in a small handmade net bag made of green nylon fishing tackle
- one metal top-piece for a shoe with various indented signs and numbers
- a picture book on the massacres at Katinka
- a black fur coat
- a black and blue enamel pendant
- a floppy doll in dark brown plastic with a frightened expression
- a giant bubble blowing toy with a rabbit lid
- a wind-up alarm clock
- a book with instructions for sewing clothes for overweight women
- illustrated cards with recipes
- one plate with red and gold decorative rings
- one painted tin for storing milk-based sweets
- one small glass bottle used for medical leeching
- one plastic fashion ring possibly made by prisoners
- one painted glass gherkin to hang on a Christmas tree

On the first day of the Museum-University we meet at a small restaurant near the History Museum. We have been to the market and are coming together for the first time. A short while later we set up our "lab" backstage on the top floor of the museum in a temporary exhibition space. We spend several hours looking at the different objects and discussing them, each purchaser explaining why they bought what they did. We decide to place three tables at the entrance to the museum. These tables and the twenty-odd chairs are retrieved from the disused café area of the museum. In the same dark area near the toilets in the museum's basement is a new depot: the gathering ground for objects sent in by people from the frontline of Ukraine's war. Shrapnel, shards, and oddly formed artifacts are placed on surfaces waiting to be inventorised.

I can't read the texts in the museum, but I'm told that they present a particular perspective on Ukraine's history, something that is far from neutral. None of the texts are translated into a second language. But luckily there are more objects than texts: neat displays and quasi heraldic constellations of photographs and old utensils, carriages, agricultural implements, and reconstructions of bourgeois homes. In one room a man plays the piano, in another, a woman in nineteenth century dress smiles attractively and begins to describe the environment on display. In nearly every room a woman of fifty plus sits calmly in the corner on an easy chair, handbag placed on her lap, watching the visitors. Sometimes she's arranged the space to accommodate her needs: a window is partially open to let in a light breeze, a mirror lies on a sill, a book or a drink is at hand. She turns the lights on as visitors enter the room. It's a dense and exhausting experience for most of them. The director explains to me that *Excursi* or guided tours leave people shattered. She has divided the entrance ticket by departments so one can visit less at one time.

Around the table at the Museum-University we discuss national and "common" knowledge. I question migrancy and collections. What happens when a visitor does not share the "common" knowledge but brings another set of references to the experience? Is this ignorance to be corrected? Are members of the public in danger of misreading an essential ingredient of Ukrainian historical facticity? What hierarchical subtext underlies the difference between a national citizen of Ukraine and a nonnational, foreign visitor? For whom is this museum intended today? What was "common" knowledge during the Soviet period and what is it in today's "globalized" world?

Four years later, in the summer of 2019, with my students from the University of Arts and Design in Karlsruhe, I tested out a second model for a Metabolic Museum-University or MM-U. We squatted the exhibitions of the 33rd Ljubljana Biennial of Graphic Arts as well as the city's major museums. The seven days of the week were altered from Monday, Tuesday, Wednesday, Thursday and so forth to Lungday, Tongueday, Eyeday, Skinday, Liverday, Brainday, and Heartday. Repurposed director's chairs were fitted with tongue-shaped tables and shelves with mini-beamers that provided visitors with the chance to sit down and *spam the hang* by projecting their own visual references in between exhibits. Our faculty was built primarily from graduate students researching in different fields, ranging from anthropology, neuroscience, and image theory to feminist art histories. In retrospect, I wondered whether we had placed emphasis on certain organs to the detriment of others, conjoining institutional renditions of gender, class, race, and colonialism with conceptions of the human body. Today, the substantive organ, be it the lungs, heart, liver, kidneys, or genitals, occupies biopolitical, economic, and social concerns. Yet one might consider returning to premodern notions of metabolism, defining health and, by this conceit, art and its agency, through fluid substances and humors secreted by bile, blood, and phlegm.

These two models of the Museum-University demonstrate that the solution for an inclusive institution built on past conditions requires humble tests, exercises, and rehearsals. Remediation is not about reappropriating colonial spoils safeguarded in obsolete imperial institutions. It is a process of self-reflexive and critical assessment that necessitates careful and respectful interaction with different agents willing to renegotiate the authority of the host. To do this, architectonic structures have to be put in place that support both analogue and digital work on these collections. The ultimate model may require the construction of a new space of education within the museum that is indissociable from its exhibitions and collections. Such a hybrid venue requires all the necessary technical configurations to make possible in-depth inquiry into artifacts and archives.[108] This Museum-University banks on the unmonetized research collection of past and its potential to inform new epistemological alliances that contradict and aggravate the normativity of inherited disciplines and their genealogies. Today a legal argument to enable rights of access to these vast so-called ethnographic collections for researchers of all nations, cultures, and schools of thought urgently needs to be developed. Only with the provision of access can one generate a museum of the commons and with it, an equitable reassessment of colonial collections whilst they are still stored in Europe. To reconsider the energy-generating functions of these venues would be a first step toward constructing conditions that take into account the contemporaneity of the world's manifold art histories.

In Frankfurt, the museum and laboratory were conceived as fifty percent inquiry and fifty percent curation, with equal parts private and public qualifying the organicist character of the exhibitions. The laboratory procedure helped to identify and retrieve objects that had fallen out of power. This, in turn, generated critical conversations within a post-ethnological framework. In such a manner it became possible to suspend the common obsession with masterpieces of so-called tribal art that perpetuates a lineage necessarily derived from nineteenth-century taste and values. The exhibitions *Object Atlas*, *Trading Style*, *Foreign Exchange*, and *El Hadji Sy* engaged audiences, but they also required visitors to suspend expectations. And these were, as very often in such museums, the desire to be transported back to the enigma of exoticism that had once generated the relationship of a particular artifact to another culture and its people.

Access to former colonial collections not only helps to define radically diasporic spaces of learning for future generations, it has the potential to activate sheltering structures for artists, scientists, historians, and students enabling them to meet, exchange, learn, and develop contemporary knowledge together. Here the metabolic indicates self-assembly with pathways that interconnect and flow through organic and non-organic formations. A metabolic process transforms and decenters, recycles, and energizes expectations and understandings of the formation of aesthetic practices. No longer should anything be seen in isolation, but each inquiry becomes a reflection of temporary interdependencies between artworks, people, objects, media, equipment, experiences, observations, laws, economies, and affects. Be they obliquely related or even incongruous, such alliances can be pertinent enough to initiate new relations between forms of art and emergent meanings, challenging the monopolies of the museum and university to produce and control new diasporic imaginaries.

If the museum is an unfinished enterprise consolidated through European imperialist representation, then the ultimate vector today needs to be the human being in an emancipatory and ecological dialogue with the existence of everything that this venue and its collections provide and invoke: a museum without condition, to paraphrase Jacques Derrida.[109] Such an open, untethered location with no vantage points or attempts to direct the mind toward the confines of one elucidation or another would be a field, an expanse, an agronomy where every visitor would farm modest meanings from unmastered works, slowly apprehending the metabolics of the museum as a body.

Manifesto for Rights of Access to Colonial Collections Sequestered in Western Europe
Dakar, May 2018

Where are we now?
Twenty-six years since the first edition of Dak'Art,
the Biennial of Visual Arts in Senegal.
Twenty-six years since Alpha Oumar Konaré,
former president of Mali and president of ICOM, stated:
"that it's about time that we questioned
the fundamental basis of the situation
and killed—I repeat killed—the Western model
of the museum in Africa in order for new methods
for the conservation and promotion
of our heritage to flourish."

Let's think back to these colonial museums
1863: Saint-Louis in Senegal,
and the museum of "Tropical Africa"
created by Louis Faidherbe
in the service of the French Republic;
1907: Windhoek, Namibia,
and the museological structure set up by colonial Germany;
1910: Nairobi, Kenya and Lagos, Nigeria,
and the museums founded by British imperialism.

And one century later, in 1966,
in the throes of post-independence,
the Musée Dynamique of Léopold Sédar Senghor,
that *dynamythical* museum opens in Dakar.
(Rest in peace!)
And with it, all the desire for internationalism,
for festivals, gatherings, and workshops,
those manifestations at the Village des Arts in Dakar,
the artists' collectives of Tenq and Huit Facettes,
and the infamous Laboratoire Agit-Art!
(Rest in peace!)

And slowly, but far too slowly,
the issue is raised today of collections in Europe,
engendered by imperialism and the market,
by noxious colonialism with its sinister discourse,
and serial kleptomania.
These collections locked up still today in the vaults
of the ethno-colonial museums of Western Europe.

Intellectual and governmental plantations!
Notions of imperialist progress!
The monoculture of ethnology!
Disciplinary and discursive closure!
Taxonomies and scientific racism!
Metabolisms covered in blood!
"Colomentalities!"
(Rest in peace!)

What to do today with the mass of what are called "objects"?
Objects in collections that are named "ethnographic,"
"object-witnesses," in the words of Marcel Griaule,
"objects" from the market in "tribal art"?
These millions of artifacts!
An inordinate quantity in Europe alone.
All without author!
Without intellectual rights!
Incarcerated by ethnology and its genealogies,
which originate, more often than not,
outside the countries of origin,
identified by collecting, resales,
and swapping between museums.
A provenance at home in the salons
and "secret gardens" of "patrons,"
from Nelson Rockefeller
to Marc Ladreit de Lacharrière.

All these objects in inaccessible depots!
Under the Seine in Paris,
where sleep in the holdings
of ships built for slavery,

these muted bodies,
these human remains.
Or otherwise, secreted in the urban periphery,
in the "prison house of radical difference
and negativity" (Simon Gikandi),
in that fridge-freezer of the soul,
confined because of their double or triple toxicity,
as carriers of microbiome, capable of
unleashing unexpected pandemics,
or so they tell us ...

Necropolitics of sequestered objects!
Hyper-restrictive access!
Discursive claustrophobia!
Exerting control!
Control!
Control over future interpretations!
Because anything is possible if you omit
the artist,
the author,
the producer,
the name of the undocumented,
to replace it with *ethnos*.

Where are we now?
Restitution?
Yes, please!
Provenance research?
Yes, please!
Retrace the biographies of objects acquired or stolen?
Yes, please!
Find out what those object hunters and
organ poachers of the Other excluded?
Yes, please!
But where?
With whom?
With what?
Ah okay!
So, reify omission instead?

Return to the source,
bring back the handmaidens of colonialism,
the priests of ethnological phantasmagoria,
encourage their hermeneutic labor once more,
restore the legitimacy of their discipline,
just as they were about to go into retirement ...
Not sure?
No thanks!

That's when the European state magnanimously walks in,
hand in hand with the universal museum
of the twenty-first century!
Now, go get a visa to visit your heritage
in Paris, Berlin, Brussels, London, Amsterdam, or Vienna!
Framed by a display fashioned by interior design,
exclusive and expulsive.
An exhibition that only adds a sentence or two ...
Because that's the point!
They didn't document much
on those colonial collecting expeditions, did they?
Instead, it was
Collect! Collect! Collect!

Ah, the excoriation of the name of the engineer,
the artist, the architect!
And the bombs of World War II
that destroyed the archives!
The fires in the reserves ...
We know them all too well.
Yet, what a relief for biographical analysis.
What comfort for the status of the "masterpiece."
But then, how to heal the colonial wound?
"Kill the museum!" declared Alpha Konaré.

Hold on! We insist upon restitution!
But not blindly, at the pace of a snail.
We won't wait for ethnological resuscitation
and the organ trade to restore the ghosts of the past.
We won't wait for the discourse of provenance,

with its polite politics,
step by step,
piece by piece.
We have to act now, while restitution is underway
And push for legislation between museums,
for the rights of access
to the art histories of the worlds, held in
the British Museum in London
the Musée du Quai Branly in Paris
the Humboldt Forum in Berlin
the Tropenmuseum in Amsterdam
the Royal Museum for Africa in Brussels
the Weltmuseum in Vienna.
Open up those bunkers!
And revise these collections,
while they are still in Europe.
Dare to radically rethink the condition of the museum,
and begin with the deepest of injuries,
where no redemption exists for the intermediary:
the curator.

Let's build Museum-Universities!
Physical and conceptual spaces for remediation,
with an architecture made for healing
and reinterpreting these agent-objects.
Let's face their stubborn materiality,
which has been so terribly neglected.
Build incongruous and problematic assemblages,
and yes, integrate digitalization.
But wait a minute!
Who will select what is to be digitalized?
Who will access these material worlds
knowingly hidden and forgotten,
if not the priests of ethnology and the market?
And, let's not forget the parameters of conservation!
That ideology of material survival,
which is remarkably impenetrable,
with its longue durée of a thousand years or more.

No more monocultures!
No more intellectual plantations!
No more museum mimicries!
No more aesthetic hegemonies!
No more object hierarchies!
No more museological pyramids!
That "absent air conditioning,"
those "inadequate conservators,"
etcetera, etcetera ...

Let's take control of these reservoirs of ingenuity!
And change the ergonomy of museums,
those "orgone accumulators" of consumerism.
Build spaces for inquiry
with rooms for conceptual intimacy,
sites for transborder art production
and disciplinary transgression
centered on these anxious and contested collections.
Museum-Universities to welcome the new
generation of students and researchers
more diasporic than ever before.
With their politics of communication
and future transitional methodologies.
So that, with patented prototypes,
based on these occluded historical collections,
they can rename the excluded authors,
and return both respect and copyright
back to their ancestors!
Organs and alliances!

All of you!
Artists!
Writers!
Curators!
Filmmakers!
Lawyers!
Architects!
Ecologists!
Brothers and Sisters!
There is no time to lose!

Notes

Prologue

1 Ann L. Stoler, *Duress. Imperial Durabilities in Our Times* (Durham, 2016). In the preface, Stoler indicates how "colonial presence" is manifest in both "tangible" and "intangible" forms, hence her script for the "(post)-colonial."

Walking Through

2 Robert Harbison, *Eccentric Spaces* (Cambridge, MA, 1977/2000), p. 147.
3 Diana Fuss and Joel Sanders, "An Aesthetic Headache: Notes from the Museum Bench," in *Interiors*, eds. Johanna Burton, Lynne Cooke, and Josiah McElheny (Berlin, 2012), p. 65.
4 Ibid., pp. 69–70.
5 Ibid., p. 72.
6 Ibid., p. 75.
7 Ciraj Rassool aptly points out that ethnographic collections are "genocidal collections." Conversation with the author, January 2019.
8 Paul B. Preciado, "Inside the Museum's Body," in *The Beast and the Sovereign*, eds. Hans D. Christ, Iris Dressler, Paul B. Preciado, Valentín Roma (Leipzig, 2018), p. 101.
9 Ibid.
10 Stoler 2016 (see note 1), p. 7.
11 Felwine Sarr and Bénédicte Savoy, "The Restitution of African Cultural Heritage. Toward a New Relational Ethics." Report commissioned by French president Emmanuel Macron, November 2018, pp. 42–47.
12 Achille Mbembe at the closing keynote speech of the MoMA conference "The multiplication of perspectives," April 28, 2019, The Museum of Modern Art, New York, https://www.moma.org/calendar/events/5429 (accessed May 7, 2019).
13 Issa Samb in conversation with the author, Dakar, March 23, 2010.

Artists and Anthropologists

14 "Maculate" is a term Ann L. Stoler used to describe anthropology in a paper given at the annual Adolf Jensen lecture series in the spring of 2014 at the Frobenius Institute in Frankfurt.

15 James Clifford and George E. Marcus, *Writing Culture: The Poetics and Politics of Ethnography* (Berkeley, 1986/2010).
16 Joseph Kosuth, "The Artist as Anthropologist," in *The Fox*, No.1, (New York, 1975). Reprinted in Joseph Kosuth, *Art after Philosophy and After. Selected Writings 1966–1990* (Cambridge, MA, 1991), pp. 117–24.
17 Ibid.
18 As Bob Scholte wrote, "What seems to me to be urgently required is a genuinely dialectical position, one in which 'analytical procedures (and descriptive devices are chosen and) determined by reflection on the nature of the encountered phenomena and on the nature of that encounter' (Fabian, 1971). This would mean that every procedural step in the constitution of anthropological knowledge is accompanied by radical reflection and epistemological exposition. In other words, if we assume a continuity between experience and reality, that is, if we assume that an anthropological understanding of others is conditioned by our capacity to open ourselves to those others (Huch, 1970), we cannot and should not avoid the 'hermeneutic circle' (Ricoeur, 1971), but must explicate, as part of our activities, *the intentional processes of constitutive reasoning*, which make both encounter and understanding possible." (my italics). Kosuth 1975 (see note 16), p. 26.
19 I am grateful to Wolfgang Stengel for having documented this moment.
20 Clémentine Deliss, ed., *Object Atlas. Fieldwork in the Museum*, exh. cat. Weltkulturen Museum, Frankfurt am Main (Bielefeld, 2011), p. 394.
21 "In anthropology, it ought to be time to sacrifice the individualism as the subject position that has been at the core of anthropology's approach to research, publication, pedagogy, and, above all, thinking." Paul Rabinow, *The Accompaniment. Assembling the Contemporary* (Chicago, 2011), p. 202.
22 Michael Oppitz in conversation with the author, Berlin, March 5, 2018.
23 See Clémentine Deliss, *Seven Stories about Modern Art in Africa*, exh. cat. Whitechapel Gallery (Paris, 1995).
24 The practice of painter and curator El Hadji Sy (*1954, Dakar) represents a conceptual and aesthetic nerve within post-independence African art. Exhibited internationally since the late seventies, he is equally known for his defiant attitude toward state cultural policy. In 1977, he took charge of an army barracks on Dakar's waterfront. This became the first iteration of the Village des Arts, a creative hub for seventy artists, actors, musicians, filmmakers, and writers. There, in 1980, he founded the multidisciplinary project space Tenq, a Wolof term that signifies articulation, and continued to remodel this curatorial dialogue in other locations during the eighties and nineties. The international workshops that he organized under the same name in Saint Louis du Senegal (1994) and in Dakar (1996) enabled new networks to be forged between artists working in continental Africa and Europe at a time when digital communications and social media were

nonexistent. To do this, El Hadji Sy reclaimed a disused Chinese worker's camp near Dakar's airport and turned it into a second Village des Arts. As an active player of the Laboratoire Agit-Art since the collective's foundation in the mid-seventies, Sy was responsible for its visual staging and costumes as well as its strategic interpellation of Senegalese cultural politics. He was an originator of the interventionist artists' group Huit Facettes, whose work in rural Senegal was presented at Documenta 11 in Kassel in 2002. See Clémentine Deliss and Yvette Mutumba, eds., *El Hadji Sy: Painting, Performance, Politics*, exh. cat. Weltkulturen Museum Frankfurt am Main (Zurich, 2015).
25 *Primitivism in 20th Century Art: Affinity of the Tribal and the Modern*, exh. cat. The Museum of Modern Art (New York, 1984).
26 Friedrich Axt and El Hadji Sy, eds., *Anthology of Contemporary Fine Arts in Senegal* (Frankfurt, 1988).
27 See Wole Soyinka, *Beyond Aesthetics. Use, Abuse, and Dissonance in African Art Traditions*, (Ibadan, 2020), p. XX.
28 See the writings of Chika Okeke-Agulu in particular *Postcolonial Modernism: Art and Decolonisation in Twentieth-Century Nigeria*, (Durham, 2015). See also the exhibition and publication by Okwui Enwezor, *The Short Century: Independence and Liberation Movements in Africa 1945-1994*, (Munich, 2001).
29 See Deliss and Mutumba 2015 (see note 24). The exhibition was cocurated with Philippe Pirotte, who also wrote an essay for the publication.

Blind Spots

30 Paul Rabinow, *French Modern. Norms and Forms of the Social Environment* (Chicago, 1988), pp. 353–54.
31 See Clémentine Deliss, *Exoticism and Eroticism: Representations of the Other in Early Twentieth Century French Anthropology*, Ph.D diss. (unpublished), (School of Oriental and African Studies, University of London, 1988).
32 Alpha Oumar Konaré, former president of Mali and then-president of ICOM, stated in ICOM's 1992 message from the president, "it is about time that we questioned the fundamental basis of the situation and 'killed'—I repeat, killed—the Western model of the museum in Africa in order for new methods for the conservation and promotion of our heritage to flourish."
33 Paul Rabinow and Anthony Stavrianakis, *Demands of the Day. On the Logic of Anthropological Inquiry* (Chicago, 2013), p. 85; see also Rabinow, *Marking Time: On the Anthropology of the Contemporary* (Princeton, 2008).
34 Paul Rabinow, *The Accompaniment: Assembling the Contemporary* (Chicago, 2011), p. 111.
35 *Lotte or the transformation of the object*, on view at Steirischer Herbst, Kunsthaus Graz, 1990, and at the Academy of Fine Arts, Vienna, 1991.
36 See Susan Vogel, ed., *Africa Explores. 20th Century African Art*, exh. cat. Museum for African Art and The New Museum of Contemporary Art (New York, 1991).

Spatial Taxonomies

37 The jury included anthropologists and sociologists Paul Rabinow, James Clifford, and Richard Sennett; curator Peter Pakesch and the artist Thomas Struth. Architects David Adjaye, Nikolaus Hirsch, Andras Palffy, Peter Cheret, Louise Hutton, Marcel Meili, Michael Schumacher, Bettina Götz, Adolf Krischanitz, Nieto Sobejano, Tony Fretton, Bruno Fioretti Marquez, and Gigon Guyer all took part and contributed to the ideas and plans for the new museum building. Kuehn Malvezzi won the competition.

The Archival Underbelly

38 See Clémentine Deliss and Yvette Mutumba, eds., *Foreign Exchange, (or the stories you wouldn't tell a stranger)*, exh. cat. Weltkulturen Museum Frankfurt am Main, (Zurich, 2014).

39 Ibid., p. 163.

40 Opening speech by Bernhard Hagen, founding director of the Museum für Völkerkunde, 1904. Archives of the Weltkulturen Museum, Frankfurt am Main.

41 Deliss and Mutumba 2014 (see note 38).

First Guests

42 Carol Becker, Achim Borchardt-Hume, and Lisa Yun Lee, eds. *Theaster Gates* (London, 2015), p. 12.

43 Gates reutilizes found materials from the properties he occupies, makes artworks from them, and reinvests part of the returns back into his collective institution. Each marble bond, produced in an edition of one hundred, was sold for five thousand euros at the Art Basel fair.

44 See Romi Crawford, "Theaster Gates and the Centripetal Force of Archives," in *Theaster Gates/black archive*, exh. cat. Kunsthaus Bregenz (Bregenz, 2017), p. 83.

45 Becker, Borchardt-Hume, and Lee, 2015 (see note 42), p. 20.

46 Jyotindra Jain recorded by the author at the meeting organized by the Wissenschaftskolleg zu Berlin and IEARN, held in New Delhi, May 4, 2011.

47 Ibid.

Laboratories and Workshops

48 "When I split up with Mick and left with Nicholas, I took a beautiful Persian carpet and some Ossie Clark dresses and all my Deliss silk clothes. So these were the clothes I was wearing when I was living on the street, a wraith-like vision, an anorexic waif, feeling no pain, and not feeling any cold either, of course, you see, because of the smack." Marianne Faithful, *Memories, Dreams & Reflections* (London, 2008), p. 8.

49 "The Schaulager concept was devised by Maja Oeri for the art collection of the Emanuel Hoffmann Foundation. The starting point was the idea that interaction with the original work is essential to the study of art. Storing works openly guarantees their accessibility for viewers, scholars and restorers." https://www.schaulager.org/en/schaulager/concept (accessed March 22, 2020).

50 See Clémentine Deliss, "Portable Homelands. From Field to Factory," in *Hello World. Revising a Collection*, exh. cat. Hamburger Bahnhof–Museum für Gegenwart (Munich, 2018), p. 259

Agency and Collections

51 "An epistemic object: a knowledge generator in one way or the other," Hans-Jörg Rheinberger, speaking at *100 Years of Now. The Opening* at Haus der Kulturen der Welt, Berlin, September 30, 2015.
52 "The object of an ostensive definition remains there, whatever happens to the index of the onlooker. But the object of a performative definition vanishes when it is no longer performed—or if it stays, then it means that other actors have taken over the relay. And this relay, by definition, cannot be 'the social world,' since it is that very world which is in dire need of a fresh relay." Bruno Latour, *Reassembling the Social. An Introduction to Actor-Network Theory* (Oxford, 2005), pp. 37–38.
53 "An intermediary, in my vocabulary, is what transports meaning or force without transformation: defining its inputs is enough to define its outputs.... Mediators, on the other hand, cannot be counted as just one; they might count for one, for nothing, for several, or for infinity. Their input is never a good predictor of their output; their specificity has to be taken into account every time. Mediators transform, translate, distort, and modify the meaning or the elements they are supposed to carry.... it is this constant uncertainty over the intimate nature of entities—are they behaving as intermediaries or as mediators?—that is the source of all the other uncertainties we have decided to follow." Ibid., p. 39
54 Paul Rabinow, preface to *Object Atlas, Fieldwork in the Museum*, Deliss 2015 (see note 20).
55 "Controversies about agencies have to be deployed to the full, no matter how difficult it is so as not to simplify in advance the task of assembling the collective." Latour 2005 (see note 52), p. 50.
56 Jacques Derrida, "The Future of the Profession or the University without Condition (Thanks to the 'Humanities' What Could Take Place Tomorrow)," in *Jacques Derrida and the Humanities, A Critical Reader* (Cambridge, 2002), pp. 24–26. "For this implies the right to do it performatively, that is, by producing events, for example by writing, and by giving rise to singular oeuvres (which up until now has been the purview of neither the classical nor the modern Humanities)." p. 26.
57 Peter Osborne in Deliss and Mutumba 2014 (see note 38).
58 Conversation with Oppitz (see note 22).
59 The exhibition *Parapolitics - Cultural Freedom and the Cold War* on view at the Haus der Kulturen der Welt in Berlin in 2017-18 aimed to reveal the cultural underpinnings of the CIA, which according to the curators' research was behind the successful organization of artists' clubs such as Mbari and Oshogbo in Nigeria.

60 See Paul Rabinow, *French Modern* (Chicago, 1995).
61 Hubert Fichte, *Psyche Glossen, Die Geschichte der Empfindlichkeit*, (Frankfurt am Main, 1990), p. 34.
62 See Antje Majewski, *La Coquille, Conversation entre Issa Samb et Antje Majewski, Dakar 2010*. http://www.antjemajewski.de/portfolio/la-coquille-conversation-entre-issa-samb-et-antje-majewski-dakar-2010-2010/ (accessed March 22, 2020).
63 See Clémentine Deliss, *Exoticism and Eroticism: Representations of the Other in Early French Anthropology*, Ph.D. diss (unpublished), (University of London, 1988).
64 "Poussière," entry in *Documents*, No.5, October 1929, p.2.

Experiments in Transgression

65 *Metronome*, No.0 (Dakar) 1996; *Metronome* No. 1 (London), 1997; *Metronome* No.2 (Berlin), 1997; *Metronome* No.3 'Tempolabor' (Basel), 1998; *Metronome* No.4-5-6 'Backwards Translation' (Frankfurt, Vienna, Bordeaux, Edinburgh, Biella), 1999; *Metronome* No.7 'The Bastard' (Copenhagen, Oslo, Stockholm, Bergen, Malmö), 2001; *Metronome* No.9 'Le Teaser' (Paris), 2005 including Metronome Press; *Metronome* No.10 'Future Academy—Shared, Mobile, Improvised, Underground, Hidden, Floating' (Portland), 2006; *Metronome* No.11 'What is to be done,' (Tokyo), 2007. Two special issues of *Metronome* were produced for *Documenta* 12 magazines: *Metronome* No. 10, coedited with artist Oscar Tuazon, a survivalist guide to future art academies with tips on mobile living and getting by with minimum expenditure; and *Metronome* No. 11, a bilingual Japanese-English edition on translation, mobility, and future faculties of knowledge in art academies. Connected to *Metronome* was *Metronome Press* in Paris, codirected by Clémentine Deliss and Thomas Boutoux between 2005 and 2007.
66 Exceptions are Michel Leiris, *L'Afrique Fantôme* (Paris, 1934); Bronislaw Malinowski, *A Diary in the Strict Sense of the Term* (Palo Alto, 1967); and Paul Rabinow, *Reflections on Fieldwork in Morocco* (Berkeley, 1977).
67 In 2000, Chantal Crousel invited me to show at her gallery with Rirkrit Tiravanija and Alenka Pirman.
68 Claude Prosper Jolyot de Crébillon, *The Sofa*, in *The Libertine Reader: Eroticism and Enlightenment in Eighteenth-Century France* (New York, 1997) p. 281.
69 For an expansive presentation of *Future Academy*, see Clémentine Deliss, "Roaming, Prelusive, Permeable," in Steven Henry Madoff, ed., *Art School (Propositions for the 21st Century)* (Cambridge, MA, 2009).
70 I researched this through the exhibition *Seven Stories about Modern Art in Africa* back in 1995, looking into the relationships between colonial art education and civic infrastructures in various African metropoles. See *Seven Stories about Modern Art in Africa*, exh. cat. Whitechapel Gallery (Paris, 1995).

71 Paul Rabinow, "On the Anthropology of the Contemporary," Frazer Memorial Lecture, 2008. YouTube video, 45:08, uploaded by Prof Alan Macfarlane - Ayabaya, November 20, 2008, https://www.youtube.com/watch?v=jDGywEGyJog (accessed March 22, 2020).
72 Otobong Nkanga in *Foreign Exchange (or the stories you wouldn't tell a stranger)*, Deliss and Mutumba, 2014 (see note 38).

A Museum in Reverse

73 James Clifford, *Returns. Becoming Indigenous in the Twenty-First Century* (Cambridge, MA, 2013), p. 43.
74 Michael Oppitz, in *Object Atlas, Fieldwork in the Museum*, Deliss 2015 (see note 20), p. 408.
75 Tom McCarthy, *Satin Island* (London, 2015), p. 3.
76 Ibid., p. 13.
77 Ibid., p. 20–21.
78 Ibid., p. 33.
79 Ibid., p. 96.
80 Interview with Clémentine Deliss, January 2013.
81 This was the working title of what later became *Foreign Exchange (or the stories you wouldn't tell a stranger)*, (see note 38).
82 Concept drafted by resident artist Luke Willis Thompson, 2013.
83 See note 80.
84 Luke Willis Thompson in Deliss and Matumba 2014 (see note 35), p. 231–ff.
85 Peter Osborne in Deliss and Matumba 2014 (see note 38), p. 183.

86 Achille Mbembe goes straight to the point when he states that the debates surrounding the restitution of looted artifacts coincide disturbingly with the intensification of the arrest, detention, and subsequent repatriation of human beings in the transnational European fight against illegal immigration.
87 Jacques Derrida, *The Spectres of Marx: The State of the Debt, the Work of Mourning, and the New International* (New York and London, 1994), p. 149.
88 Michael Taussig, *My Cocaine Museum* (Chicago, 2009), p. 267.
89 "Le hazard, dans mes mains, vint placer l'objet du monde le plus ambigu. Et les reflexions infinies qu'il me fît faire, pouvaient aussi bien me conduire à ce philosophe que je fus, qu'à l'artiste que je n'ai pas été." Paul Valéry, "EUPALINOS ou l'Architecte," in *La Nouvelle revue française*, 1921. Translation by the author.
90 Christina Sharpe, *In the Wake. On Blackness and Being*, (Durham, 2016), p. 15.
91 Simon Gikandi, keynote speech, Dak'Art conference, Cheikh Anta Diop University, May 2018.
92 "In the wake, the semiotics of the slave ship continue: from the forced movements of the enslaved to the forced movements of the migrant and the refugee, to the regulation of Black people in North American streets and neighborhoods, to those ongoing crossings of and drownings in the Mediterranean Sea, to the brutal colonial reimaginings of the slave ship and the ark; to the reappearances of the slave ship in everyday

life in the form of the prison, the camp, and the school." Sharpe 2016 (see note 90), p. 21.

93 Paul B. Preciado in *Organs & Alliances*, 2018, produced as a limited-edition offline-only portfolio with students from the ENSAPC in Paris, and the Hochschule für Grafik und Buchkunst in Leipzig.

94 Frédéric Keck states: "At the Musée du quai Branly, the priority attributed to ethnographic objects is not based on their materiality but their value in the art market .... This is where I see an analogy with the stockpiling of medication in preparation for a pandemic. The value of the objects is reclassified in relation to their exposure to risk." See the conversation between Clémentine Deliss and Frédéric Keck in "Occupy Collections." In *South as a State of Mind*, No. 7, Documenta 14 No. 2, Spring/Summer 2016.

Vital Relationships

95 Sebastian Schellhaas, ed., *Die Welt im Löffel (The World in a Spoon)* (Bielefeld, 2012).

96 In *The Function of the Orgasm*, 1927, Wilhelm Reich claims that by building an accumulator, one can redirect the orgone energy of sexual pleasure and heal neurosis. The ethnographic museum's desire to capture, possess, and classify life's unknowns projects an unspoken erotics of transgression and possession onto the ritual artefact.

97 See Slavoj Žižek in *Metronome* No. 2 (Berlin), 1997.

98 The option of a funeral by the fading of light—as a form of final respect—was proposed by resident writer Gabriel Gbadamosi for the exhibition and catalogue *Foreign Exchange (or the stories you wouldn't tell a stranger)* (see note 38).

99 Theodor W. Adorno, *Prisms*, trans. Samuel and Shierry Weber, Neville Spearman, (London, 1967), p. 177.

100 Preciado 2018 (see note 8), p. 101. See also note 93.

101 Stoler 2016 (see note 1), p. 9.

102 G. E. Davie, *The Crisis of the Democratic Intellect* (Edinburgh, 1986), p. 15. See also Davie, *The Democratic Intellect* (Edinburgh, 1961).

103 Murdo MacDonald, internal paper, *Future Academy*, Edinburgh, 2005.

Models of a Museum-University

104 See Bruno Latour, *Où atterir? Comment s'orienter en politique?* (Paris, 2017).

105 Sarr and Savoy (see note 11).

106 Ivan Illich, *Deschooling Society* (New York, 1971), p. 34.

107 Joseph Beuys and Frans Haks, *Das Museum* (Wangen, 1993).

108 For example, the vacant space that epitomizes the central area in a painting show, or the flows between sculptural elements in a classic modernist gallery, may be occupied by visual interlocutors and incongruous objects. Furniture extends beyond the normative vitrine or the solitary bench. The chair and table act to dislodge patterns of intellectual classification.

109 Derrida 2002 (see note 56).

Colophon

Managing editor
Lena Kiessler

Project management
Anja Tschörtner

Copyediting
Kimberly Bradley

Graphic design
Neil Holt

Typeface
Arnhem

Production
Vinzenz Geppert

Printing and binding
GRASPO CZ, A.S.

Published by
Hatje Cantz Verlag GmbH
Mommsenstraße 27
10629 Berlin
www.hatjecantz.de
A Ganske Publishing Group Company

Co-produced with KW Institute for Contemporary Art **KW**

ISBN 978-3-7757-4780-6 (Print)

ISBN 978-3-7757-4801-8 (eBook)

Printed in the Czech Republic

MIX
Paper from responsible sources
FSC® C002795